Passing PTLLS Assessments

Passing PTLLS Assessments

Ann Gravells

Learning Matters

First published in 2010 by Learning Matters Ltd

British Library Cataloguing in Publication Data
A CIP record for this book is available from the British Library.

ISBN: 978 1 84445 378 8

This book is also available in the following ebook formats:

Adobe ebook ISBN 978 1 84445 685 7
EPUB ebook ISBN 978 1 84445 684 0
Kindle ISBN 978 1 84445 983 4

Cover design by Topics – the Creative Partnership
Project management by Deer Park Productions, Tavistock, Devon
Typeset by Pantek Arts Ltd, Maidstone, Kent
Printed and bound in Great Britain by Bell & Bain Ltd, Glasgow

Learning Matters Ltd
33 Southernhay East
Exeter EX1 1NX
Tel: 01392 215560
info@learningmatters.co.uk
www.learningmatters.co.uk

Mixed Sources
Product group from well-managed
forests and other controlled sources
www.fsc.org Cert no. TT-COC-002769
© 1996 Forest Stewardship Council
FSC

CONTENTS

ACKNOWLEDGEMENTS

The author would like to thank the following for their support and encouragement whilst writing this book.

Jennifer Clark
Peter Frankish
Bob Gravells
Alison Hodgson
Laura Rudd
Susan Simpson
Amy Thornton
Jacklyn Williams

The staff and learners of the teacher/training department at Bishop Burton College.

Ann Gravells is a lecturer in teacher training at Bishop Burton College in East Yorkshire. She has been teaching since 1983.

She is a consultant to City & Guilds for various projects as well as externally verifying the City & Guilds teacher training qualifications.

Ann holds a Masters in Educational Management, a PGCE, a degree in education, and a City & Guilds Medal of Excellence for teaching. She is the author of

- *Preparing to Teach in the Lifelong Learning Sector*
- *Principles and Practice of Assessment in the Lifelong Learning Sector*
- *Delivering Employability Skills in the Lifelong Learning Sector.*

She is co-author of

- *Planning and Enabling Learning in the Lifelong Learning Sector*
- *Equality and Diversity in the Lifelong Learning Sector*

and has edited

- *Study Skills for PTLLS.*

Ann is a Fellow of the Institute for Learning.

The author welcomes any comments from readers; please contact via her website: www.anngravells.co.uk

In this chapter you will learn about:

● the structure of the book and how to use it;

● preparing for your assessments;

● written assessments and guidance for evidencing competence.

The structure of the book and how to use it

This book has been specifically written for anyone working towards the Preparing to Teach in the Lifelong Learning Sector (PTLLS) Award at either level 3 or 4. The book is designed to help you assess the skills and knowledge you already have, in preparation for your formal assessments. The assessment criteria (Appendices 1 and 2) will help you determine an appropriate level of achievement which should be discussed and agreed with your assessor. If you are aiming to achieve at level 4 you will need to carry out relevant research, reference your work to theorists and use an academic style of writing.

The book builds upon information in the companion textbook by Gravells (2008), *Preparing to Teach in the Lifelong Learning Sector*, and Williams (2010), *Study Skills for PTLLS*. These books will help you to understand the theory and practical requirements of being a teacher in the Lifelong Learning Sector, and the academic skills required to respond to the assessment activities.

Awarding Organisations take different approaches to assessment; however, the content of the PTLLS Award does not change. Throughout your assessments, whether they are formal assignments, questions, professional discussions with your assessor or another appropriate method, you will need to demonstrate that you have met all the PTLLS Award assessment criteria at the appropriate level. The difference between the levels is expressed in the assessment criteria – the learning outcomes remain the same.

This book will suit anyone taking the PTLLS Award, whether you are taking a short intensive programme of study, attending a formal programme over a number of weeks, or taking a distance, open or blended learning approach. The PTLLS Award can be achieved as a unit in its own right, or as part of the Certificate or Diploma in Teaching in the Lifelong Learning Sector, or the Certificate in Education/Post Graduate Certificate in Education. It can be delivered and assessed in a number of ways; however, the assessment criteria must be met whichever approach is taken. The PTLLS Award is usually a 60-hour programme: 30 hours include contact with your teacher, assessor and peer group, and 30 hours are classed as self-study time. This time should be used for reading, research and working towards the assessment activities. You may find it beneficial to complete a reflective learning journal after each session you attend and/or teach while you are working towards your PTLLS Award. You may be issued with a pro-forma for this once you have commenced the programme, or you could use a diary to reflect on what you have learnt and how you intend to put theory into practice. There is a pro-forma in Appendix 10 if you would like to use it.

Chapters 1–5 contain self assessment questions for each of the five learning outcomes of the PTLLS Award. The assessment criteria for each level are shown in boxes. You can work through the questions as you progress through your programme of study and they can be completed in the order which suits your learning.

You can then compare your responses with the guidance. This will help you to demonstrate and evidence your competence towards each learning outcome of the PTLLS Award. Additional guidance is given towards level 4 achievement. The book is not intended to give you the answers to questions you may be asked in any formal assessments; your responses will be specific to you, the subject you teach, and the context and environment in which you teach. The book will, however, guide you through the PTLLS Award criteria with a view to helping you focus upon the requirements of the assessments.

Chapter 6 will help you plan and prepare for your micro-teach session whether you are pre-service or in-service. All learners taking the PTLLS Award must deliver a 15- or 30-minute session either to their peer group (pre-service) or their own learners (in-service). A visual recording may be taken of this: viewing it will enable you to reflect upon your delivery and see things you perhaps weren't aware of. You will also gain information regarding giving and receiving feedback, and evaluating your delivery.

Chapter 7 contains useful information regarding the PTLLS Award along with the main Awarding Organisations' assessment requirements together with an explanation of the assessment methods you are likely to experience.

The appendices contain the criteria and self-audits at levels 3 and 4 which will help you track your progress towards the PTLLS Award assessment criteria, together with completed examples of evidence you can provide. There are also hints and tips for the micro-teach session and a rationale pro-forma to help you plan a scheme of work and micro-teach session. The peer observation and feedback pro-forma will help you give constructive and developmental feedback to your peers, which forms part of the PTLLS Award assessment criteria. There is also a self-evaluation pro-forma to help you evaluate your micro-teach session. If you are a pre-service learner, you could use the scheme of work and session plan pro-formas to plan how you would deliver your subject. You will need to obtain a syllabus for your subject, many of which can be obtained from a relevant Awarding Organisation's website. If you are an in-service learner, you will need to check with your organisation which forms they require you to use. All pro-formas referred to in this book are available via the Learning Matters website.

Preparing for your assessments

As a starting point and to check the level you feel you could achieve, carry out an initial assessment by completing the self-audit in Appendices 1 or 2. These list the PTLLS Award learning outcomes and assessment criteria at level 3 and level 4 respectively, and by completing this self-audit, you will identify the level most suited to you. Read through each and note any evidence you currently have which covers the outcomes, along with the work you need to do to meet those left blank. Your evidence might be in the form of written responses or reference to documents such as a session plan or handout. It doesn't matter if you have lots of blank spaces at the moment; you are still learning and may not yet know how to achieve all the criteria. Once you have worked through the learning outcomes in Chapters 1–5, have another look and see if you can complete the blank spaces.

To start the process of achieving your PTLLS Award, you will need to enrol at a training organisation, college or other establishment which offers it. If you are currently teaching (in-service), your employer may arrange this for you; if you are not yet teaching (pre-service), you will need to find out where the PTLLS Award is offered and apply for a place. A quick search via the internet or a phone call to your local training organisation will soon locate these. You will need to be knowledgeable, experienced and/or qualified in a suitable subject that you would like to teach. You might be interviewed (in person or on the telephone) and/or have to complete an application form (paper-based or electronic). At this stage it would be useful to ask any questions or discuss any concerns you might have before you start. Check with your interviewer if they know of any specific requirements or qualification you need to teach your subject.

Once you have enrolled, you will either attend formal sessions or follow another learning approach. Other approaches include blended learning, which combines different methods; for example, completing activities online via the internet or working at home with occasional attendance at group sessions. As you progress through your programme of study, you can work through the self-assessment questions in Chapters 1–5. These will help you focus upon the assessment criteria and guide you through the PTLLS Award learning outcomes. As you gain the skills and knowledge required, you will need to carry out various assessment activities, which will be issued to you at the training organisation you have enrolled with. These will differ depending upon which Awarding Organisation you are taking the qualification with. They will usually consist of theory assessments which will test your knowledge of teaching and learning, and practical assessments which will test your ability to teach learners. The latter will be by delivering a short session, 15 or 30 minutes, known as a 'micro-teach'. This will be to your current learners if you are in-service, or to your peers who are attending the PTLLS Award programme if you are pre-service, and will be observed by your teacher or assessor.

You will have a designated teacher and/or assessor at the training organisation who will assess your work and give you ongoing support and feedback. If you don't pass any assessments first time, known as a 'refer', you should be given the opportunity to discuss it with your assessor or have another attempt. The activities in this book will help you understand the PTLLS Award criteria and prepare you for the assessments: they are not a substitute for any formal assessments you will be given. If you are an in-service teacher, you should be assigned a mentor in the same subject area that you are teaching who should be able to give you ongoing help, support and advice.

After completing each chapter (from Chapters 1–5), you could write a reflective learning journal to help you appreciate your development so far towards each learning outcome. You can then fill in any blank areas you might have on the self-audit form (Appendix 1 for level 3, Appendix 2 for level 4). When you enrol with an organisation to take the PTLLS Award, you will need to check that you are registered for the correct level of achievement.

Written assessments and guidance for evidencing competence

Chapters 1–5 contain the questions and guidance for each of the five learning outcomes of the PTLLS Award. You may like to work logically through each section or just concentrate on the assessment criterion which relates to learning outcome of the section you are currently studying.

When answering the questions, make sure your responses are specific to the subject you are teaching, your learners and the context and environment within which you teach (if you are in-service). If you are not currently teaching (pre-service), answer the questions hypothetically as to what subject and where you would like to teach.

Examples of the context might include work-based learning, further education, sixth form college, adult and community learning, offender learning, the forces, etc. Examples of the environment include classrooms, workshops, community halls, etc. If you are in-service, you can make reference to documentation you use at work along with relevant policies, procedures and guidelines that you follow.

You need to respond appropriately to the level you are working towards. For example, if the assessment criteria include the word 'explain' then you need to describe *what* you have done. If it is 'justify', you will need to describe *what* you have done and *why* you did it that way. If you are aiming for level 4, you will need to use academic writing and referencing. Please refer to Williams (2010), *Study Skills for PTLLS*, for guidance regarding this. Advice for achieving at level 4 is given in the guidance sections of Chapters 1–5.

Once you have completed the questions, check your responses with the guidance. This is designed to help you focus upon the requirements of the PTLLS Award assessment criteria.

Summary

In this chapter you have learnt about:

- the structure of the book and how to use it;

- preparing for your assessments;

- written assessments and guidance for evidencing competence.

Theory focus

Books

Gravells A (2008) *Preparing to Teach in the Lifelong Learning Sector* (3rd edition). Exeter: Learning Matters

Williams J (2010) *Study Skills for PTLLS.* Exeter: Learning Matters

Websites

Awarding Organisations – www.ofqual.gov.uk/607.aspx

Institute for Learning – www.ifl.ac.uk

Lifelong Learning UK – www.lluk.org

CHAPTER 1
UNDERSTAND OWN ROLE, RESPONSIBILITIES AND BOUNDARIES OF ROLE IN RELATION TO TEACHING

This chapter is in two parts. The first part, **self assessment questions**, contains activities which relate to the first learning outcome of the PTLLS Award: '*Understand own role, responsibilities and boundaries of role in relation to teaching*'. The assessment criteria are shown in boxes and are followed by questions for you to answer. Ensure your responses are *specific to you*, the *subject you would like to teach* and the *context* and *environment* in which you will teach. After completing all the questions, check your responses with the second part: **Guidance for evidencing competence**. The guidance is not intended to give you the answers to questions you may be asked in any formal assessments; however, it will help you focus your responses towards meeting the PTLLS Award requirements.

Self assessment questions

> Level 3 – 1.1 Explain own role and responsibilities, and boundaries of own role as a teacher
>
> Level 4 – 1.1 Review own role and responsibilities, and boundaries of own role as a teacher

Q1 Explain or review what you consider your role to be. You might like to think of this in relation to the training cycle or the teaching and learning cycle.

Q2 Explain or review your responsibilities as a teacher.

Q3 Explain or review the boundaries you may encounter as a teacher.

> Level 3 – 1.2 Identify key aspects of relevant current legislative requirements and codes of practice within a specific context
>
> Level 4 – 1.2 Summarise key aspects of relevant current legislative requirements and codes of practice within a specific context

Q4   What guidelines, regulations, codes of practice and/or legislation must you follow to teach your subject in your organisation?

Q5   Identify or summarise the key aspects of these.

Level 3 - 1.3 Identify other points of referral available to meet the potential needs of learners

Level 4 – 1.3 Review other points of referral available to meet the potential needs of learners

Q6   List a few examples of potential needs of learners.

Q7   Identify or review a few points of referral to meet these needs.

Level 3 – 1.4 Identify issues of equality and diversity, and ways to promote inclusion

Level 4 –1.4 Discuss issues of equality and diversity, and ways to promote inclusion

Q8   What do the terms equality, diversity and inclusion mean?

Q9   Identify or discuss some issues of equality and diversity that you might encounter.

Q10 Identify or discuss ways to promote inclusion with your learners.

Level 3 – 1.5 Explain the need for record keeping

Level 4   1.5 Justify the need for record keeping

Q11 What types of records will you need to maintain as a teacher?

Q12 Explain or justify the need for keeping these records.

Guidance for evidencing competence

Level 3 – 1.1 Explain own role and responsibilities, and boundaries of own role as a teacher

Level 4 - 1.1 Review own role and responsibilities, and boundaries of own role as a teacher

Q1 Explain or review what you consider your role to be. You might like to think of this in relation to the training cycle or the teaching and learning cycle.

The training cycle consists of:

- identifying needs (of learners and organisation, initial assessments);
- planning (scheme of work and session plans);
- designing (resources, presentations, handouts and activities);
- facilitating (teaching and learning approaches, supporting learners);
- assessing (checking performance and knowledge, giving feedback);
- evaluating (learners, programme, external requirements and own continuing professional development (CPD)).

The teaching and learning cycle is similar to the training cycle and consists of:

- identifying needs (of learners and organisation, initial assessments);
- planning (scheme of work, session plans and resources);
- enabling (teaching and learning approaches, using resources, presentations, handouts and activities, supporting learners);
- assessing (checking performance and knowledge, giving feedback);
- quality assurance and evaluation (learners, programme, external requirements and own CPD).

Terminology in education is constantly evolving but your role as a teacher will always involve the above activities. You will need to state how you will carry out all the duties related to each aspect of the training or learning cycle, as well as engaging and motivating learners, communicating effectively with learners and others and promoting inclusion. You will also need to state how you create a safe and positive learning environment. Your role, however, will not only be to teach; you may find yourself coaching, counselling, training, assessing, mentoring, encouraging and supporting your learners as and when necessary. You need to maintain a professional relationship with your learners and follow organisational protocols and relevant codes of practice. It helps if you are well organised, enthusiastic and passionate about your subject, as this will be conveyed to your learners through your teaching methods. It is always useful to have a contingency plan in case anything doesn't go as you had planned.

At level 4 you will need to review your role and refer to theorists such as Kolb's (1984) Learning Styles and Maslow's (1954) Hierarchy of Needs as part of your response to this. You will also need to review all aspects of the training or learning cycle, discussing in detail what your role is and how and why you perform it.

Q2 Explain or review your responsibilities as a teacher.

You will need to explain your responsibilities such as being knowledgeable regarding your specialist subject and remaining up to date with any new developments. Taking part in CPD activities will help ensure this. You need to be aware of relevant guidelines, codes of conduct and legislation relating to your subject, the context within which you teach and your organisation. You need to prepare your sessions to include all learners; keep records such as the register; maintain assessment grades; and give appropriate support to your learners. Your responsibilities might also include interviewing learners, following up absences, checking equipment, producing resources and attending meetings and events. It might be your responsibility to undertake a Criminal Records Bureau (CRB) check to allow you to work with young people and vulnerable adults.

At level 4 you will need to review how your responsibilities affect your role and your learners; for example, what would happen if you didn't carry out your responsibilities adequately? You could also refer to codes of practice such as the Institute for Learning (IfL) Code of Professional Practice which came into force in April 2008 and covers the areas:

- integrity;
- respect;
- care;
- practice;
- disclosure;
- responsibility.

Q3 Explain or review the boundaries you may encounter as a teacher.

Boundaries are all about knowing your own limits professionally and personally. Explaining the ones you encounter may vary depending upon your learners, your subject and the type of organisation you are working in. You might telephone a learner if they have been absent, but making several calls would be inappropriate. You should remain professional at all times and not get personally involved; for example, not joining learners' social networking sites if asked. You should avoid touching learners inappropriately or giving extra support to some learners and not to others. You need to remain in control, be fair and ethical with all your learners and not demonstrate any favouritism towards particular learners.

Other boundaries include:

- culture;

- deadlines;

- environment;

- lack of resources;

- management demands;

- policies and procedures;

- syllabus requirements.

At level 4 you will need to review what your boundaries are (as above) and state what you would or would not do in specific circumstances. For example, if you had a learner who was experiencing financial problems, you would advise them to seek specialist help. You would not discuss their income and expenditure with them or advise them to take out a loan.

> Level 3 – 1.2 Identify key aspects of relevant current legislative requirements and codes of practice within a specific context
>
> Level 4 – 1.2 Summarise key aspects of relevant current legislative requirements and codes of practice within a specific context

Q4 What guidelines, regulations, codes of practice and/or legislation must you follow to teach your subject in your organisation?

These will differ depending upon your subject, the context and environment within which you teach, but will include generic aspects such as the following.

- Apprenticeship, Skills, Children and Learning Act 2009.

- Awarding Organisation guidelines.

- Children Act 2004: Every Child Matters.

- Copyright Designs and Patents Act 1988.

- Criminal Records Bureau clearance.

- Data Protection Act 1998 amended 2003.

- Disability Discrimination Act 1995, amended 2005.

- Education and Skills Act 2008.

- Equality Act 2006.

- Health and Safety Act 1974.

- Inspection requirements (Ofsted, etc.).

- Organisational guidelines such as dress, timekeeping.

- Organisational policies and procedures such as appeals, complaints, risk assessments.

- Professional codes of conduct such as the Institute for Learning Code of Professional Practice (IfL).

- Safeguarding Vulnerable Groups Act 2006.

- The Further Education Teachers' Qualifications (England) Regulations 2007 (QTLS/ATLS status).

There will be aspects relevant to your subject which you will need to ascertain. For example, the Control of Substances Hazardous to Health (COSHH) Regulations 2002, if you work with hazardous materials, or the Display Screen Regulations 1992, if you work with computers. There will also be aspects relevant to your organisation; for example, the appeals and complaints procedures.

Q5 Identify or summarise the key aspects of these.

One example is Identified below; you will need to research the ones you have referred to in your response to question 4.

The Children Act 2004 provides the legal underpinning for the Every Child Matters: Change for Children programme. 'Well-being' is the term used in the Act to define the five Every Child Matters outcomes which should be incorporated into teaching, namely:

- be healthy,

- stay safe;

- enjoy and achieve;

- make a positive contribution;

- achieve economic well-being.

At level 4 you will need to go into greater detail with your responses by summarising them. For example, you would give examples of how you would incorporate the above five outcomes when teaching your subject.

> Level 3 – 1.3 Identify other points of referral available to meet the potential needs of learners
>
> Level 4 – 1.3 Review other points of referral available to meet the potential needs of learners

Q6 List a few examples of potential needs of learners.

Some potential needs you may encounter include learning difficulties and disabilities; behaviour; language; physical; emotional; dyslexia; dyspraxia; etc. You may also encounter learners with financial, health, housing or other personal problems. If you are not an expert with any potential needs you should refer your learners to an appropriate specialist.

Q7 Identify or review a few points of referral to meet these needs.

Identified points of referral will be internal to your organisation; for example, learning support staff, basic skills support staff and counsellors. There will also be external points of referral; for example, appropriate people or agencies such as Job Centre Plus, the Citizens Advice Bureau, doctors, etc.

At level 4 you will need to review where the people or agencies are based; for example, their address, telephone number, website details, etc., along with what they can do to help your learners, and the processes in place at your organisation to refer your learners as necessary.

> Level 3 – 1.4 Identify issues of equality and diversity, and ways to promote inclusion
>
> Level 4 –1.4 Discuss issues of equality and diversity, and ways to promote inclusion

Q8 What do the terms 'equality', 'diversity' and 'inclusion' mean?

Equality is about the rights of learners to have access to, attend, and participate in their chosen learning experience. This should be regardless of ability and/or circumstances. Inequality and discrimination should be tackled to ensure fairness, decency and respect among learners. Equal opportunity is a concept underpinned by legislation to provide relevant and appropriate access for the participation, development and advancement of all individuals and groups. In the past, equality has often been described as *everyone being the same* or *having the same opportunities*. Nowadays, it can be described as *everyone being different, but having equal rights*.

Diversity is about valuing and respecting the differences in learners, regardless of ability and/or circumstances, or any other individual characteristics they may have. If you have two or more learners, you will experience diversity. You are also different from your learners in many ways, and they are different from each other; therefore they are entitled to be treated with respect, with their differences taken into consideration. You may have a mixed group of learners with different levels of experience who are aiming to achieve the same qualification but at a different level. You could therefore set different activities and targets for the different assessment criteria.

Inclusion is about involving all your learners, treating them all equally and fairly, without directly or indirectly excluding anyone.

Q9 Identify or discuss some issues of equality and diversity that you might encounter.

Identified issues could include prejudice, discrimination and stereotyping between learners, all of which you should challenge with your learners as they occur. Incorporating activities based around equality and diversity and the local community and society within which your learners live, could help your learners' understanding. You may have learners of different levels within your group and setting different targets and activities will help them achieve these. You may also encounter learners with sensory impairments, mobility difficulties, cancer, epilepsy, diabetes, HIV or multiple sclerosis. If you are aware of any learner needs, you will be able to support them, or refer them to a relevant specialist.

To ensure you comply with the Equality Act 2006, you need to be proactive in all aspects of equality and diversity, and make sure your teaching style and resources promote and include all learners in respect of the six strands:

- age;
- disability;
- gender;
- race;
- religion and belief;
- sexual orientation.

At level 4 you will need to discuss the issues you have identified in detail and state what you would do in each situation and why. For example, how you would identify if a learner has any additional needs and what you would do to support them.

Q10 Identify or discuss ways to promote inclusion with your learners.

Identified ways to promote inclusion with your learners include ensuring your delivery and resources represent the six strands of legislation. You could also make sure your learners have access to facilities, resources and equipment which are appropriate for the subject. All learners are entitled to dignity and respect; even though you will experience many different attitudes, values and beliefs you should not impose your own upon others, or allow other learners to. You could carry out activities and discussions with your learners to challenge discriminatory behaviour and respect confidentiality. All learners should be involved in the learning process and be encouraged to communicate and work with each other. You should also ensure the language and jargon you use are at an appropriate level. You should use a variety of different teaching styles to adapt to the needs of all your learners.

At level 4 you will need to discuss these in more detail and give examples of how you would promote inclusion with your learners; for example, through discussions. You should relate your answers to relevant legislation and/or organisational guidelines and policies, and relevant theories of learning and motivation such as Knowles (1978) and Maslow (1954).

Level 3 – 1.5 Explain the need for record keeping

Level 4 – 1.5 Justify the need for record keeping

Q11 What types of records will you need to maintain as a teacher?

These may differ at your organisation but will mainly include application forms, interview records, initial assessments, registers, individual learning plans or action plans, schemes of work, session plans, progress and tutorial reviews, assessment grades, minutes of meetings and standardisation, internal verification/moderation records, CPD etc.

Q12 Explain or justify the need for keeping these records.

Explaining why records must be maintained will include organisational, awarding and regulatory requirements. Records are usually kept for three years and can be asked for by inspectors and verifiers/moderators. All records should be legible, confidential and secure.

At level 4 you will need to justify the reasons for keeping certain records and state the organisations or regulatory bodies who necessitate them and why. You could also state what would happen if you did not keep records and mention confidentiality and the Data Protection Act 1998 and 2003.

Theory focus

Books

Gravells A (2008) *Preparing to Teach in the Lifelong Learning Sector* (3rd edition). Exeter: Learning Matters

Gravells A and Simpson S (2009) *Equality and Diversity in the Lifelong Learning Sector.* Exeter: Learning Matters

HMI (2004) *Every Child Matters: Change for Children.* London: DfES

Kolb DA (1984) *Experiential Learning: Experience as the Source of Learning and Development.* New Jersey: Prentice-Hall

Knowles MS (1978) *The Adult Learner; A Neglected Species*, (2nd edition). Gulf Publishing

Maslow AH (1954) *Motivation and Personality.* New York: Harper

Wallace S (2007) *Teaching, Tutoring and Training in the Lifelong Learning Sector* (3rd edition). Exeter: Learning Matters

Williams J (2010) *Study Skills for PTLLS.* Exeter: Learning Matters

Websites

Apprenticeships, Skills, Children and Learning Act 2009 – www.opsi.gov.uk/acts2009/ukp99_20090022_en_1

Children Act 2004: Every Child Matters – www.everychildmatters.gov.uk

Copyright Designs and Patents Act (1988) – www.opsi.gov.uk/acts/acts1988/UKpga_19880048_en_1.htm

Control of Substances Hazardous to Health (COSHH) – www.hse.gov.uk/COSHH/index.htm

Criminal Records Bureau (CRB) – www.crb.gov.uk

Data Protection Act 1998 and 2003 – regulatorylaw.co.uk/Data_ Protection_Act_2003.html

Disability Discrimination Act 1995 amended 2005 – www.opsi.gov.uk/Acts/acts2005/ukpga_20050013_en_1

Display Screen Regulations (1992) – www.opsi.gov.uk/si/si1992/Uksi_ 19922792_en_1.htm

Education and Skills Act 2008 – www.dcsf.gov.uk/educationandskills

Equality Act 2006 – www.opsi.gov.uk/acts/acts2006/pdf/ukpga 20060003 _en.pdf

Equality and Diversity Forum – www.edf.org.uk

Fleming's learning styles – www.vark-learn.com

Health and Safety at Work Act 1974 – www.hse.gov.uk/legislation/hswa.htm

Honey and Mumford learning styles – www.peterhoney.com

Institute for Learning – www.ifl.ac.uk

Ofsted – www.ofsted.gov.uk

Safeguarding Vulnerable Groups Act 2006 – www.opsi.gov.uk/ACTS/acts2006/ukpga_20060017_en_1

The Further Education Teachers' Qualifications (England) Regulations 2007 – www.opsi.gov.uk/si/si2007/uksi_20072264_en_1

Theories of learning – www.learningandteaching.info/learning/

CHAPTER 2
UNDERSTAND
APPROPRIATE TEACHING
AND LEARNING
APPROACHES IN THE
SPECIALIST AREA

This chapter is in two parts. The first part, **Self assessment questions**, contains activities which relate to the second learning outcome of the PTLLS Award: '*Understand appropriate teaching and learning approaches in the specialist area*'. The assessment criteria are shown in boxes and are followed by questions for you to answer. Ensure your responses are *specific to you*, the *subject you would like to teach* and the *context* and *environment* in which you will teach. After completing all the questions, check your responses with the second part: **Guidance for evidencing competence**. The guidance is not intended to give you the answers to questions you may be asked in any formal assessments; however, it will help you focus your responses towards meeting the PTLLS Award requirements.

Self assessment questions

> Level 3 – 2.1 Identify and demonstrate relevant approaches to teaching and learning in relation to the specialist area
>
> Level 4 – 2.1 Identify, adapt and use relevant approaches to teaching and learning in relation to the specialist area

Q13 What teaching and learning approaches do you plan to use for your specialist subject? *You will then need to demonstrate these as part of a teaching session or micro-teach.*

Q14 What resources do you plan to use?

> Level 3 – 2.2 Explain ways to embed elements of functional skills in the specialist area
>
> Level 4 – 2.2 Evaluate a range of ways to embed elements of functional skills in the specialist area

Q15 What are functional skills and why have they been introduced?

Q16 Explain or evaluate how you would embed elements of functional skills in your specialist subject area.

> Level 3 – 2.3 Justify selection of teaching and learning approaches for a specific session
>
> Level 4 – 2.3 Evaluate the teaching and learning approaches for a specific session

Q17 State the teaching and learning approaches you have used for a specific session; for example, your micro-teach.

Q18 Justify or evaluate why you chose these.

Guidance for evidencing competence

Level 3 – 2.1 Identify and demonstrate relevant approaches to teaching and learning in relation to the specialist area

Level 4 – 2.1 Identify, adapt and use relevant approaches to teaching and learning in relation to the specialist area

Q13 What teaching and learning approaches do you plan to use for your specialist subject? *You will then need to demonstrate these as part of a teaching session or micro-teach.*

This will very much depend upon the subject you are teaching, and the context and environment you are teaching in. However, you should choose aspects which will engage, stimulate and motivate your learners. You should always consider your learners when choosing the teaching and learning approaches you will use; it's not about what *you* will teach, but how *they* will learn. As individuals learn in different ways and have different levels of experience and knowledge, you will need to take these into consideration when planning your sessions. Whether you are teaching individuals or groups will determine the approaches you take. For example, individual coaching in sports subjects, group work in a classroom, or distance learning for those taking an online programme whom you might not meet face to face. If you teach or coach on a one-to-one basis, you will have more time to dedicate to individual requirements and might cover more work in greater depth with them than in a group environment. Do be aware of attention spans and learning styles and take into consideration aspects of differentiation, health and safety, equality and diversity and the five outcomes of Every Child Matters, which are:

- be healthy;
- stay safe;
- enjoy and achieve;
- make a positive contribution;
- achieve economic well-being.

You might want to use a variety of teaching and learning approaches and consider the advantages and disadvantages of each of these beforehand.

Example approaches include:

- coaching;
- demonstrations;
- discussions;

- formal delivery of theory;

- group work;

- online learning;

- practical activities;

- presentations;

- research;

- role plays;

- seminars;

- simulations;

- use of information and communication technology (ICT).

A mixture of different approaches within your sessions will ensure you meet all learning styles and help retain learner engagement and motivation. If you plan to use group activities, consider which learners will work together in case learners with strong personalities dominate and change the group dynamics. Equally, make sure the quiet learners don't get left out of activities and are able to participate. You might like to decide who will work with whom, or use paired activities. Don't be afraid of trying something different; for example, giving your learners responsibility for part of a session, encouraging peer assessment or using fun activities. If you do use a learner-centred rather than a teacher-centred approach, you will need to be confident in the way you manage the activities, and also be able to deal with any behavioural issues as they arise.

You will need to be aware of any challenges and barriers to learning that your learners may have; for example, a lack of confidence or a fear of embarrassment in front of their peers. There may also be barriers to effective teaching and learning such as the seating layout in your room being inappropriate, the room being too hot or cold or not big enough to accommodate all your learners. You may need to liaise with others to resolve any issues. However, you will need to take them into consideration when planning the approaches you will use.

You will need to keep up to date with changes in your specialist subject area and have an awareness of current developments; an example is ICT which is continually evolving. You may need to request the purchase of new resources or equipment prior to teaching; there might not be a budget for this at your organisation, therefore you might need to improvise. You should also be using the latest qualification syllabus to plan your scheme of work.

At level 4 you should be using a variety of approaches to meet the individual needs of your learners and be able to relate these to theories. You could refer to examples such as: visual, aural, read/write and kinaesthetic learning (VARK), as noted by Fleming (2005); activist, pragmatist, theorist and reflector learning styles, as noted by Honey and Mumford (1992); and learning through the senses of sight, hearing, touch, smell and taste, as noted by Laird (1985). You should be setting different tasks to stretch and challenge higher-level learners, which should be planned for in your scheme of work and session plans. You could mention Knowles (1978), who is the theorist who brought the concept of adult learning to the fore. He has argued that adulthood takes place when people behave in adult ways and believe themselves to be adults. Most formal education still focuses on the teacher as the provider of knowledge (pedagogy) rather than the learner being at the centre of the learning process (andragogy). Using an andragogical approach encourages active learning rather than passive learning, with you as the teacher acting as a facilitator. However, the approach you take will very much depend upon the subject you are teaching. Taking a pedagogical approach will not suit all learners and may make them switch off from the learning process. You might also consider which domain you want to reach; for example, Bloom's (1956) cognitive, affective and psycho motor domains. Think of cognitive as the head, i.e. knowledge, affective as the heart i.e. feelings, and psychomotor as the hands, i.e. skills. You should also take Maslow's (1954) Hierarchy of Needs into account, as not all learners will have the opportunity to have the lower-level needs met at home, therefore affecting their learning when they are with you.

Q14 What resources do you plan to use?

This will very much depend upon the subject you are teaching, the context and environment you are teaching in and the level of learners you are teaching.

Some examples are:

- audio/visual equipment;

- computerised presentations;

- computers;

- flipchart paper and pens;

- handouts;

- interactive whiteboards;

- overhead projector;

- physical resources, models and apparatus;

- textbooks;

- worksheets, puzzles or crosswords.

If you teach a practical subject, you might use specialist equipment and will need to ensure these have been properly serviced or tested and meet any health and safety requirements. All resources used should be appropriate in terms of level, quality, quantity and content and be relevant to the subject and the learning expected. Handouts and presentations should be checked for spelling, grammar, punctuation and sentence construction errors. You should also ensure that the text and pictures represent all aspects of society.

At level 4 you will need to adapt resources; for example, redesigning a handout or a presentation based upon feedback from your learners or your own evaluation after the last use. You will need to state what you will adapt and the reasons why you will do this.

> Level 3 – 2.2 Explain ways to embed elements of functional skills in the specialist area
>
> Level 4 – 2.2 Evaluate a range of ways to embed elements of functional skills in the specialist area

Q15 What are functional skills and why have they been introduced?

Functional skills consist of English, maths and information and communication technology (ICT). They provide essential knowledge, skills and understanding that will enable learners to operate confidently, effectively and independently in life and at work. Functional skills were introduced by the government in 2007 as part of the reform of 14–19 and adult education to equip the United Kingdom with the skills it needs for the twenty-first century. You may identify some of your learners who need extra support with these skills and you will need to know who in your organisation you could refer them to. You might also feel your own skills in these areas need to be improved, therefore you could do further training yourself. If you are not competent, you will not set a good example to your learners. As you progress through further teaching qualifications you will need to demonstrate your skills in the minimum core of language, literacy, communication and ICT.

Q16 Explain or evaluate how you would embed elements of functional skills in your specialist subject area.

You will need to explain how you can embed English, maths and ICT within your sessions.

Examples include:

- English – reading, writing, listening, speaking, discussions;

- maths – approximations, estimations, calculations, measurements;

- ICT – use of email, web-based research, word processing of assignments and reports, using spreadsheets, databases and presentation packages.

To explain how you will do this you will need to give specific examples which relate to your specialist subject. An example for cookery would be:

- English – reading and discussing recipes, writing a list of ingredients, listening to the teacher and asking questions, talking to other learners;

- maths – calculating weights and costs of ingredients, measuring amounts, estimating calorific values, cooking times and temperatures;

- ICT – using a word processor to type up a menu, researching healthy eating websites, emailing other learners.

At level 4 you should evaluate how you would embed elements of functional skills within your specialist subject. You could experiment with different opportunities for each of English, maths and ICT and then evaluate them by assessing the success or otherwise of the activities you used. Asking your learners how they felt will give you valuable feedback, enabling you to take a different approach next time if necessary.

> Level 3 – 2.3 Justify selection of teaching and learning approaches for a specific session
>
> Level 4 – 2.3 Evaluate the teaching and learning approaches for a specific session

Q17 State the teaching and learning approaches you have used for a specific session; for example, your micro-teach.

The teaching and learning approaches you actually used for your session might be different from those you originally planned to use (see questions 13 and 14). This is fine as it shows you are taking your learners' needs into account as long as you can state why this was. You will need to state what you actually used for your specialist subject.

Q18 Justify or evaluate why you chose these.

At level 3 you will need to justify why you chose the teaching and learning approaches you used. A justification for using a demonstration with your learners would be to show them how to perform a practical task, therefore enabling them to put theory into practice after they have observed you.

At level 4 you would evaluate why you chose the approaches you did by giving more details; for example, if the majority of your learners are kinaesthetic, a practical task after a demonstration would suit their learning style best. For those learners who are read/write or visual you could issue a handout to summarise the key points and direct learners to appropriate websites or texts. For aural learners you could discuss the process and ask questions. You could also obtain feedback from your learners to evaluate how the session went and whether you were able to meet their individual needs. Always ensure you are being inclusive and addressing equality and diversity throughout your sessions. There may be factors affecting your chosen approaches such as organisational requirements, codes of practice and legislation; for example, the Health and Safety at Work Act 1974.

If you have used group activities you could refer to Tuckman and Jenson's (1977) Group Formation theory of forming, storming, norming, performing and adjourning. You could also refer to Belbin's (1993) Team Roles, or Berne's (1964) Transactional Analysis theory regarding the roles individuals take on in different situations. Being aware of these theories will help you understand why your learners act differently and what happens in group situations.

Theory focus

Books

Belbin M (1993) *Team Roles At Work*. Oxford: Elsevier Science and Technology

Berne E (1964) *Games People Play – The Psychology of Human Relationships*. London: Penguin Books

Bloom BS (ed) (1956) *The Taxonomy of Educational Objectives, The Classification of Educational Goals*. New York: McKay

Fleming N (2005) *Teaching and Learning Styles: VARK strategies*. Honolulu: Honolulu Community College

Gravells A (2008) *Preparing to Teach in the Lifelong Learning Sector* (3rd edition). Exeter: Learning Matters

Gravells A and Simpson S (2009) *Equality and Diversity in the Lifelong Learning Sector*. Exeter: Learning Matters

HMI (2004) *Every Child Matters: Change for Children*. London: DfES

Honey P and Mumford A (1992) *The Manual of Learning Styles* (3rd edition). Maidenhead: Peter Honey Associates

Knowles MS (1978) *The Adult Learner; A Neglected Species* (2nd edition). Gulf Publishing

Kolb DA (1984) *Experiential Learning: Experience as the Source of Learning and Development*. New Jersey: Prentice-Hall

Laird D (1985) *Approaches to Training and Development*. Addison Wesley

Maslow AH (1954) *Motivation and Personality*. New York: Harper

Schön D (1983) *The Reflective Practitioner*. San Francisco: Jossey-Bass

Tuckman B and Jenson M (1977) Stages of small group development. *Group and Organisational Studies*, 2(4): 419–27

Williams J (2010) *Study Skills for PTLLS*. Exeter: Learning Matters

Websites

Equality and Diversity Forum – www.edf.org.uk

Every Child Matters – www.everychildmatters.gov.uk

Fleming's learning styles – www.vark-learn.com

Functional skills – www.qcda.gov.uk/22100.aspx

Health and Safety at Work Act – www.hse.gov.uk/legislation/hswa.htm

Honey and Mumford learning styles – www.peterhoney.com

Teaching resources, support and advice – www.excellencegateway.org.uk/page.aspx?o=home

Theories of learning – www.learningandteaching.info/learning/

Tuckman – www.infed.org/thinkers/tuckman.htm

CHAPTER 3
DEMONSTRATE SESSION
PLANNING SKILLS

This chapter is in two parts. The first part, **Self assessment questions**, contains activities which relate to the third learning outcome of the PTLLS Award: '*Demonstrate session planning skills*'. The assessment criteria are shown in boxes and are followed by questions for you to answer. Ensure your responses are *specific to you*, the *subject you would like to teach* and the *context* and *environment* in which you will teach. After completing all the questions, check your responses with the second part: *Guidance for evidencing competence*. The guidance is not intended to give you the answers to questions you may be asked in any formal assessments; however, it will help you focus your responses towards meeting the PTLLS Award requirements.

Self assessment questions

> Level 3 – 3.1 Plan a teaching and learning session which meets the needs of individual learners
>
> Level 4 – 3.1 Plan a teaching and learning session which meets the needs of individual learners

Q19 Produce a scheme of work for a minimum of six sessions showing what you plan to teach in each, for your specialist subject. You can decide on the dates, times and length of the sessions.

Q20 Produce a session plan for one of the sessions from the scheme of work (if you are in-service) or for your micro-teach (if you are pre-service). The session plan should be for 15 or 30 minutes.

> Level 3 – 3.2 Justify selection of resources for a specific session
>
> Level 4 – 3.2 Evaluate how the planned session meets the needs of individual learners

Q21 What resources have you planned to use in your session?

Q22 How do you plan to meet the individual needs of your learners for your planned session? *You will need to have some information about your learners prior to your delivery.*

> Level 4 – 3.3 Analyse the effectiveness of the resources for a specific session

Q23 Justify or analyse how effective the resources were for your session (in-service or micro-teach).

Guidance for evidencing competence

Level 3 – 3.1 Plan a teaching and learning session which meets the needs of individual learners

Level 4 – 3.1 Plan a teaching and learning session which meets the needs of individual learners

Q19 Produce a scheme of work for a minimum of six sessions showing what you plan to teach in each, for your specialist subject. You can decide on the dates, times and length of the sessions.

The pro-forma you should use for your scheme of work will be given to you if you are pre-service, or it might be available in electronic format or in a handbook you were given at the beginning of the programme. There is a rationale in Appendix 7 and a pro-forma in Appendix 8 that you could use to help you create a scheme of work.

All schemes of work should show:

- programme or qualification title;
- details of the group of learners;
- venue;
- dates and times;
- number of sessions;
- length of sessions;
- aim;
- objectives or learning outcomes;
- teaching and learning activities and resources;
- opportunities to embed functional skills where possible and the Every Child Matters outcomes;
- assessment activities.

If you are in-service, you should be able to use an existing scheme of work that you have created on your organisation's documentation for a current group. If you are pre-service, you will need to create one. The content and layout of schemes of work differ between organisations; however, the format should enable you to have a clear aim of what you plan to achieve with either objectives or learning outcomes for the learners to achieve. These will come from the programme or qualification syllabus and should be cross-referenced into your scheme of work. You should be able to obtain a syllabus from a relevant Awarding Organisation website. You should state the teaching and learning activities and resources you plan to use, along with how you will assess your learners. You should also show how you will integrate the functional skills of English, maths and ICT, and how you will meet the five outcomes of Every Child Matters (ECM), often referred to as Every Learner Matters in post-16 education. These are:

- be healthy;

- stay safe;

- enjoy and achieve;

- make a positive contribution;

- achieve economic well-being.

Make sure you check all dates carefully in case there are any bank or public holidays on the dates you would normally teach. The first session should include an induction to the programme and organisation, an icebreaker and the setting of ground rules. You might also need to assess prior learning in this session, or before your learners commence. All subsequent sessions should begin with a recap of the last session and time for questions, and end with an explanation of the next session. The last session should include an evaluation activity to obtain feedback from your learners which will help you improve in future. You may need to check if you will have the same venue for all the sessions and what facilities, equipment and resources will be available. The more time you take to plan your scheme of work, the easier each individual session plan should be.

At level 4 your scheme of work should be very detailed, realistic and meticulously planned. It should show a variety of teaching and learning activities to suit all learning styles, take account of health and safety and equality and diversity. Timing should be carefully considered to ensure you are not trying to achieve too much in each session, and the sessions should follow in a logical order, which might not be in the order of the syllabus. Differentiation should be planned for, with different levels of activities and assessments to meet individual needs. Assessment activities should be formative and summative, informal and formal.

If you are in-service, you could state how internal and external inspections have impacted upon your organisation's documentation for planning teaching sessions.

Q20 Produce a session plan for one of the sessions from the scheme of work (if you are in-service) or for your micro-teach (if you are pre-service). The session plan should be for 15 or 30 minutes.

The pro-forma you should use for your session plan will be given to if you are pre-service or it might be available in electronic format or in a handbook you were given at the beginning of the programme. There is a rationale in Appendix 6 and a pro-forma in Appendix 9 that you could use to help you practise creating a session plan.

All session plans should show:

- teacher's name;

- date;

- venue;

- duration;

- subject and level/syllabus reference;

- group composition; for example, differentiation, equality & diversity, individual learning needs and learning styles;

- number of learners;

- timings;

- aim of session;

- objectives or learning outcomes;

- resources;

- teaching activities;

- learning activities;

- opportunities to embed functional skills where possible and the Every Child Matters outcomes;

- assessment activities.

If you are in-service, you might be able to use an existing session plan you have created on your organisation's documentation for a current group of learners, but you will need to discuss this with your assessor. If you are pre-service, you will need to use the one provided by your assessor. You should create a session plan for the observed aspect of the PTLLS Award, which might be either 15 or 30 minutes (check the timing with the person who will observe you). Preparing the area and clearing up will be outside of this time. If you are in-service, you may be observed teaching your current group for longer than this time and your session plan will be created from your scheme of work. If you are pre-service, your session plan could be from your scheme of work or it could be something completely different such as your hobby or an interest. You will need to discuss this in advance with the assessor who will observe you.

Your session plan should have a logical beginning, middle and end and take into account differentiation, equality and diversity, individual learning needs and learning styles. You will need to ascertain these details in advance from your learners or peer group. Your aim, the objectives or learning outcomes should be stated, with a clear breakdown of what you will do and what your learners will do, along with a good mix of activities and assessment opportunities. Timings should be stated; for example, 2.00 pm, 2.05 pm, etc., next to each activity. Alternatively you could state 5 minutes, 10 minutes, etc., for each activity. You will need to consider what resources you will use; for example, electronic presentation equipment, flipchart paper, interactive whiteboard, pens, etc. Your session plan should be realistic: don't attempt to achieve too much from either yourself or your learners. Make note of an activity you could remove if you run out of time, and also something you could add if you have spare time. It is also useful to have spare activities for learners who may finish earlier than others and to have a contingency plan in case anything goes wrong. Always end your session plan with a summary of your aim, the objectives or learning outcomes and allow time for learner questions.

You will need to have a spare copy of your session plan to give to your assessor as they will use this when observing you.

At level 4 your session plan should be very detailed, realistic and meticulously planned with careful timings. You should show how you have taken into account all your learners' individual needs, and differentiated for different levels of ability. You may have to embed the functional skills of English, maths and ICT where possible and the five outcomes of Every Child Matters. However, this will depend upon how much time you have and should be discussed in advance with your observer.

Level 3 – 3.2 Justify selection of resources for a specific session

Level 4 – 3.2 Evaluate how the planned session meets the needs of individual learners

---

Q21 What resources have you planned to use in your session?

The resources you plan to use could include electronic presentation equipment, electronic whiteboards, flipchart paper and pens, specialist equipment, projectors, televisions, etc. All resources should be checked in advance to ensure they are safe and fully operational. If you are a pre-service learner, you will need to arrive early to check the room you will be teaching in and you may need to ask your assessor in advance what is available for you to use. If you are planning to use an electronic presentation, it would be useful to email this to your assessor in advance for them to check it, in case the document you plan to use isn't compatible on the day. Any resources you use should be relevant to the subject you are teaching and the individual needs of your learners.

At level 4 you could quote from relevant textbooks regarding the different resources available to meet the needs of your learners and how you will make best use of them for your specialist subject.

Q22 How do you plan to meet the individual needs of your learners for your planned session? *You will need to have some information about your learners prior to your delivery.*

Your session plan should show how you plan to meet the individual needs of your learners which is why it is important to obtain details of your learners or peer group in advance. It could be that you have a dyslexic learner who might benefit from a different coloured background rather than white for any presentations or handouts. All learners can gain from this rather than singling out and possibly embarrassing the dyslexic learners. Handouts on a pastel background, for example, cream or lemon, reduce the glare often experienced with black on white.

Your resources should not create any barriers to learning and should be accessible to all. You might have learners of different abilities or levels within the same group, therefore you will need to plan different activities to stretch and challenge the higher-level learners. You could have different assessment activities or open questions that you will use.

Level 4 – 3.3 Analyse the effectiveness of the resources for a specific session

Q23 Justify or analyse how effective the resources were for your session (in-service or micro-teach).

After delivering your session, you will need to justify how effective the resources you used actually were. You will have received feedback from your observer and your peers which will help you with this. You will need to state why you chose the resources you did; for example, flipchart paper, pens and handouts to create an active and inclusive session which enabled all learners to participate. You might not have been able to provide enough handouts for each learner, meaning they had to share, which didn't work very well. However, you might think that the resources were effective because all learners felt able to take part and had access to a hand-out. Your own reasons might differ from the feedback you have received, as your learners might have participated and not complained, just to please you.

At level 4 you will need to analyse how effective your resources were. You could describe each of your resources, how you used them during your session and how your learners benefited from them. Take into account the feedback you have received and state what you would do differently next time and why. Perhaps you could amend a handout as there was far too much text on one page, or your presentation had too many slides and you talked too much. You could quote from relevant textbooks regarding how to adapt resources to meet the needs of your learners and your specialist subject. You could also discuss the Equality Act 2006 and state how your resources have represented the six strands of equality and diversity legislation.

Theory focus

Books

Gravells A (2008) *Preparing to Teach in the Lifelong Learning Sector* (3rd edition). Exeter: Learning Matters

Gravells A and Simpson S (2009) *Equality and Diversity in the Lifelong Learning Sector.* Exeter: Learning Matters

HMI (2004) *Every Child Matters: Change for Children.* London: DfES

Williams J (2010) *Study Skills for PTLLS.* Exeter: Learning Matters

Websites

Equality Act 2006 – www.opsi.gov.uk/acts/acts2006/pdf/ukpga_20060003_en.pdf

Every Child Matters – www.everychildmatters.gov.uk

Every Learner Matters – www.emcett.com/every_learner/index.html

Functional skills – www.qcda.gov.uk/22100.aspx

Health and Safety at Work Act 1974 – www.hse.gov.uk/legislation/hswa.htm

This chapter is in two parts. The first part, **Self assessment questions**, contains activities which relate to the fourth learning outcome of the PTLLS Award: '*Understand how to deliver inclusive sessions which motivate learners*'. The assessment criteria are shown in boxes and are followed by questions for you to answer. Ensure your responses are *specific to you*, the *subject you would like to teach* and the *context* and *environment* in which you will teach. After completing all the questions, check your responses with the second part: **Guidance for evidencing competence**. The guidance is not intended to give you the answers to questions you may be asked in any formal assessments; however, it will help you focus your responses towards meeting the PTLLS Award requirements.

Self assessment questions

> Level 3 – 4.1 Explain ways to establish ground rules with learners which underpin appropriate behaviour and respect for others
>
> Level 4 – 4.1 Analyse different ways to establish ground rules with learners which underpin appropriate behaviour and respect for others

Q24 What are ground rules and why set them?

Q25 Explain or analyse different ways of setting ground rules.

> Level 3 – 4.2 Use a range of appropriate and effective teaching and learning approaches to engage and motivate learners
>
> Level 4 – 4.2 Use a range of appropriate and effective teaching and learning approaches to engage and motivate learners

Q26 Deliver your planned session, either in-service or micro-teach. Ensure you use a range of appropriate and effective teaching and learning approaches to engage and motivate your learners

> Level 3 – 4.3 Explain and demonstrate good practice in giving feedback
>
> Level 4 – 4.3 Explain different methods of giving feedback

Q27 What is feedback and why should you give it?

Q28 Explain different methods of giving feedback to your learners or peers.

> Level 3 – 4.4 Communicate appropriately and effectively with learners
>
> Level 4 – 4.4 Demonstrate good practice in giving feedback
>
> Level 4 – 4.5 Communicate appropriately and effectively with learners

Q29 Observe one of your peers and give appropriate feedback.

Q30 As part of your taught session, how would you demonstrate appropriate and effective communication techniques with your learners? *You should inform your assessor when this will take place to ensure they can observe you.*

> Level 3 – 4.5 Reflect on and evaluate the effectiveness of own teaching
>
> Level 4 – 4.6 Reflect on and evaluate the effectiveness of own teaching, making recommendations for modification as appropriate

Q31 After you have taught your session, reflect on and evaluate how effective it was.

Q32 What did you feel were your strengths and/or areas for improvement?

Q33 What recommendations or changes would you make for the future?

Guidance for evidencing competence

Level 3 – 4.1 Explain ways to establish ground rules with learners which underpin appropriate behaviour and respect for others

Level 4 – 4.1 Analyse different ways to establish ground rules with learners which underpin appropriate behaviour and respect for others

Q24 What are ground rules and why set them?

Ground rules are boundaries, rules and conditions within which learners can safely work and learn. Examples include:

- arriving on time and returning from breaks on time;
- following health and safety regulations;
- no eating or chewing gum;
- no swearing;
- respecting each other's opinions;
- switching off mobile phones and electronic devices.

Ground rules should be negotiated to help maintain order, underpin behaviour and promote respect. They should lead to a set of guidelines regarding acceptable and unacceptable behaviour and set clear boundaries within which to work. If they are not set, problems may occur which could disrupt the session and lead to misunderstandings. Empowering learners to take ownership of the ground rules should help ensure they are all followed, leading to limited disruption within the group. Ground rules should always be negotiated with your learners rather than forced upon them; they will then feel included and motivated if they are involved, taking responsibility for them. Some ground rules might be renegotiated or added to throughout the programme; for example, changing the break time. Others might not be negotiable; for example, health and safety requirements.

Q25 Explain or analyse different ways of setting ground rules.

Ways of establishing ground rules include the teacher setting and imposing them, the learners setting and agreeing them on their own, in pairs or a group, or both the teacher and learners working together by a process of negotiation. The best method is the latter as this enables the group to recognise what is and is not acceptable, giving them a sense of ownership, responsibility and rapport building. If a learner breaks a ground rule, you may find their peers reprimand them before you need to. Enabling your learners to discuss and agree the ground rules allows for negotiation and understanding of the boundaries, rules and conditions in which to effectively work and learn. It also enables them to begin working together as a group and encourages aspects such as listening, compromise and respect for others. Ground rules that are set solely by the teacher could potentially alienate the learners and make them feel less respected.

The list of ground rules could be written on flipchart paper to be displayed on the wall each time the group meets, and/or a typed version could be given to each learner, either in hard copy or emailed. Keeping the ground rules visible throughout the sessions will act as a reminder of what is not acceptable, and enable them to be amended or added to as necessary. Always refer to the rules at the beginning of the session and when a rule is broken. For example, if a learner is late, they must be reminded that it is a requirement that all lessons start promptly, otherwise they might not make the effort to arrive on time for subsequent sessions.

At level 4 you should analyse different ways of setting ground rules; for example, you could split your learners into small groups to agree a few points, then ask the groups to collate their findings and all agree one list. A contribution should be taken from each group so that all individuals feel involved. You could supervise this and give a few ideas to help prompt them if necessary.

Other methods could include a paired discussion as part of an introduction ice-breaker activity, whereby the learners discuss and note down a few ground rules. Each pair could then double up and so on until all the pairs have formed one group. If the learners in your group have never met each other before, starting with a paired discussion can help create a bond between two people who won't then feel alone in a strange environment.

Alternatively, if you have only one learner you could talk to them about what they expect from the sessions and how you can help each other maintain a professional working relationship.

Your organisation might have some basic ground rules that should be followed by every learner; for example health and safety, in which case these could be used as a basis on which to build others.

Setting the ground rules after the icebreaker activity at the beginning of the first session is usually a good time to do it. This can then set the precedent for your learners, and referring to them in subsequent sessions is a good reminder.

If your learners attend sessions by other teachers, it is a good idea to discuss what your group has agreed with them to ensure consistency during all sessions. There may be some different ground rules due to particular subjects or health and safety requirements. You might also take your learners for several different subjects and therefore might have a core list of ground rules with some specific ones for each particular subject.

You may decide to analyse different ways based upon research you have carried out and textbooks you have read. If this is the case, always reference your work to the source of your findings.

> Level 3 – 4.2 Use a range of appropriate and effective teaching and learning approaches to engage and motivate learners
>
> Level 4 – 4.2 Use a range of appropriate and effective teaching and learning approaches to engage and motivate learners

Q26 Deliver your planned session, either in-service or micro-teach. Ensure you use a range of appropriate and effective teaching and learning approaches to engage and motivate your learners.

This is a practical task which enables you to teach a session to your current learners if you are in-service, or to your peers if you are pre-service. You should take account of your responses to questions 13 and 17 and put theory into practice. Reading Chapter 6 will also help you with regard to planning and preparing your session.

> Level 3 – 4.3 Explain and demonstrate good practice in giving feedback
>
> Level 4 – 4.3 Explain different methods of giving feedback

Q27 What is feedback and why should you give it?

Feedback is about helping someone learn from their actions or behaviour. It is not criticism, which is just a person's judgment or reaction to something, often said without careful thought. Feedback should always be given in a manner which will help your learner become more effective in the future; it should be constructive and developmental. Feedback is information and constructive opinions, not an instruction list and it will be up to the person receiving it if they wish to do anything with it. Good feedback is an offer of helpful information, not a judgment of personality, character or potential.

Q28 Explain different methods of giving feedback to your learners or peers.

Some different methods of giving feedback include:

- verbal – on a one-to-one basis, as a group, as part of a review or tutorial, or in front of others; for example, the peer group;

- written – on each learner's work and/or on a separate feedback record or checklist;

- electronically – either by email or part of an online programme or web portal.

You could research other methods and ways of giving feedback; for example, the 'praise sandwich' which consists of positive feedback, negative or constructive feedback, positive feedback. You could also elaborate on the situations or contexts in which you would give feedback, and the reasons why you would do it that way; for

- use of different resources;
- using open questions to check knowledge;
- using learners' names;
- displaying positive body language;
- keeping to your session plan timings;
- summarising the objectives;
- clearing up afterwards.

Areas for improvement might include:

- asking if anyone has any knowledge of the subject already;
- not giving a handout part way through as it disrupted the group;
- using more eye contact;
- trying not to say *erm*, *yeah* and *okay*;
- keeping jargon to a minimum;
- differentiating an activity to stretch and challenge higher-level learners;
- offering to email a copy of the presentation to everyone.

Q33 What recommendations or changes would you make for the future?

Based on your areas for improvement in response to question 32, state the recommendations or changes would you make for the future.

For example:

> *I would give a handout at the end so as not to disrupt the group during the session. I found the learners fiddled with it and started reading it as soon as I gave it out and they didn't pay attention to what I was saying.*

> *I was very focused upon keeping to the timings of my session plan so that I kept looking at it rather than at my learners. I need to use more eye contact with my learners as this would enable me to observe that they are watching what I am doing, and enable them to see that I am paying attention to them.*

> *I found that three learners in the group were able to complete the activity with ease and very quickly. Next time I will create two different versions of the activity so that one can be aimed at challenging the higher-level learners further.*

I wasn't able to give everyone a copy of the presentation as the photocopier wasn't working prior to the session. If I offer to email a copy to everyone it will give them the opportunity to look at it in their own time and address issues of sustainability. In future, I will either aim to get copies done sooner so that I am better prepared, or agree with the learners to use electronic ones to help the environment.

When you are writing your recommendations for change, you could refer to relevant reflective theorists or from textbooks or journals you have researched and read.

Theory focus

Books

Brookfield SD (1995) *Becoming a Critically Reflective Teacher.* San Francisco: Jossey-Bass

Gibbs G (1998) *Learning by doing: a guide to teaching and learning methods.* Oxford: Further Education Unit

Gravells A (2008) *Preparing to Teach in the Lifelong Learning Sector* (3rd edition). Exeter: Learning Matters

Gravells A and Simpson S (2009) *Equality and Diversity in the Lifelong Learning Sector.* Exeter: Learning Matters

Griffiths M and Tann S (1992) Using reflective practice to link personal and public theories. *Journal of Education for Teaching,* Vol 18, No 1

HMI (2004) *Every Child Matters: Change for Children.* London: DfES

Kolb DA (1984) *Experiential Learning: Experience as the Source of Learning and Development.* New Jersey: Prentice-Hall

Reece I and Walker S (2007) *Teaching, Training and Learning; A Practical Guide* (6th edition). Tyne and Wear: Business Education Publishers Ltd

Schön D (1983) *The Reflective Practitioner.* San Francisco: Jossey-Bass

Wallace S (2007) *Teaching, Tutoring and Training in the Lifelong Learning Sector* (3rd edition). Exeter: Learning Matters

Williams J (2010) *Study Skills for PTLLS.* Exeter: Learning Matters

Websites

BBC – Feedback: giving and receiving – www.bbctraining.com/onlineCourse.asp?tID=2241

Ground rules – www.learningandteaching.info/teaching/ground_rules.htm

Health and Safety - www.hse.gov.uk

Reflective practice – www.learningandteaching.info/learning/reflecti.htm

CHAPTER 5
UNDERSTAND THE
USE OF DIFFERENT
ASSESSMENT METHODS
AND THE NEED FOR
RECORD KEEPING

This chapter is in two parts. The first part, **Self assessment questions**, contains activities which relate to the fifth learning outcome of the PTLLS Award: '*Understand the use of different assessment methods and the need for record keeping*'. The assessment criteria are shown in boxes and are followed by questions for you to answer. Ensure your responses are *specific to you*, the *subject you would like to teach* and the *context* and *environment* in which you will teach. After completing all the questions, check your responses with the second part: **Guidance for evidencing competence**. The guidance is not intended to give you the answers to questions you may be asked in any formal assessments; however, it will help you focus your responses towards meeting the PTLLS Award requirements.

Self assessment questions

Level 3 – 5.1 Identify different assessment methods

Level 4 – 5.1 Review a range of different assessment methods

Q34 Identify or review a range of different assessment methods.

Level 3 – 5.2 Explain the use of assessment methods in different contexts, including reference to initial assessment

Level 4 – 5.2 Evaluate the use of assessment methods in different contexts, including reference to initial assessment

Q35 What assessment methods would you use for your specialist subject and why?

Q36 What is initial assessment and why should you use it?

Level 3 – 5.3 Explain the need for record keeping in relation to assessment

Level 4 – 5.3 Justify the need for record keeping in relation to assessment

Q37 What records should you maintain as a teacher?

Q38 Explain or justify the need for these.

Guidance for evidencing competence

Level 3 – 5.1 Identify different assessment methods

Level 4 – 5.1 Review a range of different assessment methods

Q34 Identify or review a range of different assessment methods.

Assessment methods identified include:

- assignments;
- case studies;
- examinations;
- learning journals;
- observation;
- professional discussion;
- projects;
- puzzles and quizzes;
- questions – written and oral;
- recognition of prior learning;
- self and peer assessment;
- simulation;
- tests;
- witness testimony.

There are also assessment types, which include initial (at the beginning), formative (ongoing), and summative (at the end). An example of an initial assessment could be a self-assessment (like the self-audit in Appendices 1 and 2); a formative assessment could be an ongoing learning journal (to reflect on continuing professional development), and a summative assessment could be a test or an exam (to measure success).

Assessments can be formal (for example, a test), or informal (for example, a quiz), depending upon your subject. Assessment tasks or activities will be either internal (produced by you or your organisation) or external (produced by the Awarding Organisation). You may be able to make reasonable or alternative adjustments to an assessment method or type to cater for any specific learner needs. Your organisation should be able to give you details of this; for example, allowing extra time for a partially-sighted learner to read instructions.

At level 4 you should review a range of different assessment methods to demonstrate your understanding of each. For example, assignments could be used to help learners put theory into practice and help them provide evidence of knowledge and skills. An assignment can enable the assessment of several aspects of a qualification at the same time, often known as holistic assessment. All assessments, whether written by yourself or others, should be valid and reliable. A valid method will ensure you are assessing what is meant to be assessed, and a reliable method will ensure that if the assessment was done again with a similar group of learners, you would receive similar results. Most assessments will be internally and/or externally quality assured to ensure fairness and consistency, as well as validity and reliability.

At level 4 you should quote from relevant textbooks regarding assessment, for example, Gravells (2009), *Principles and Practice of Assessment in the Lifelong Learning Sector,* or Tummons (2007), *Assessing Learning in the Lifelong Learning Sector.*

> Level 3 – 5.2 Explain the use of assessment methods in different contexts, including reference to initial assessment
>
> Level 4 – 5.2 Evaluate the use of assessment methods in different contexts, including reference to initial assessment

Q35 What assessment methods would you use for your specialist subject and why?

You have previously identified several different assessment methods, and you now need to state what methods you would use for your subject in different contexts. Examples of the context might include work-based learning, further education, sixth form college, adult and community learning, offender learning, the forces, etc. You could state the context you work in (or would like to work in) and give examples of which methods you would use. For example, you might use observation and oral questions in your learner's place of work towards practical aspects of the Certificate in Customer Service. Alternatively, you might be limited to using an examination for a theoretical subject. Although the examination might take place at the end of the programme, you could use some informal assessments such as a quiz throughout the programme to test knowledge at given points. The subject you assess (or would like to assess) may restrict the assessment methods you can use due to organisational or regulatory requirements. You will need to look at the syllabus or qualification handbook to ensure you are following the correct assessment strategy for your subject. Other examples of assessment locations include classrooms, workshops, community halls, outside spaces, etc.

At level 4 you should evaluate each of the assessment methods you have stated. This will include explaining what the method is, why, when and where you would use it, and how both you and your learners will benefit from it. As an assessor, you should standardise your decisions with other assessors to ensure you are being fair and not discriminating in any way.

Q36 What is initial assessment and why should you use it?

Initial assessment is about ascertaining if your learners have any previous knowledge or experience of the subject to be assessed, or if they have any specific requirements which need to be met during their time with you. You would use initial assessments to gain relevant information regarding your learners; for example, their learning style, or their subject skills and knowledge to be able to help them develop throughout their time with you. Initial assessments can also be used to ensure learners are applying for the correct programme and are not out of their depth by wanting to achieve a much higher level than they are currently capable of. There could be particular entry requirements for your subject and an initial assessment or interview would ascertain if these had been met. Diagnostic tests could be used to ascertain information regarding maths, English or ICT. Skills audits could be used to ascertain current knowledge for particular vocational areas. This information will help you plan your sessions to meet any individual needs and/or to arrange further training and support if necessary.

Using initial assessments helps you to identify any particular aspects which may otherwise go unnoticed and ensure you are meeting equality and diversity requirements. Some learners may be embarrassed or not wish to divulge personal information on application or initial assessment forms. You could have a quiet chat with them away from other learners to find out if they have any needs or specific requirements. If you are unsure about how to help them with anything, just ask, as they are best placed to know how you could support them. Your organisation may have specific assessments or skills tests for you to use which you could discuss, along with the reasons why.

> Level 3 – 5.3 Explain the need for record keeping in relation to assessment
>
> Level 4 – 5.3 Justify the need for record keeping in relation to assessment

Q37 What records should you maintain as a teacher?

There are many records you should maintain. These include:

- accident/incident forms;
- action plans;
- appeals;
- assessment plans;
- assessment feedback;
- assessment grades;
- assessment tracking;
- diagnostic test results;

- individual learning plans;

- initial assessment;

- interview records;

- learning styles tests;

- learning support records;

- register;

- retention, achievement and progression records;

- record of achievement;

- risk assessments;

- scheme of work;

- session plan;

- skills audits;

- syllabus or qualification handbook;

- tutorial reviews;

- verifier and moderator reports;

- worksheets.

You should also state any others you use or plan to use for your specific subject and the context within which you will teach.

Q38 Explain or justify the need for these.

When explaining the need for records you should state that this enables you to keep track of your learners' progress from when they commence to when they leave, and satisfies organisational and regulatory requirements. Records can either be electronic or manual, and should be kept for a minimum of three years.

At level 4 you should justify the need for keeping records by being specific about each record, i.e. what it is and why it is used. You also need to state the reasons they were introduced and what benefit they are to all parties concerned. You will need to find out what documents your organisation expects you to use (if you are in-service). The syllabus or qualification handbook will give you specific details regarding the assessment strategy. However, they may not provide the assessment documentation you will need. If your organisation also doesn't provide any, you might have to design your own. If you didn't keep assessment records and a learner lost their work, you wouldn't have any proof you had planned for and assessed their efforts unless you kept relevant records. You could also mention confidentiality and data protection requirements and how these relate to record keeping.

Theory focus

Books

Gravells A (2008) *Preparing to Teach in the Lifelong Learning Sector* (3rd edition). Exeter: Learning Matters

Gravells A (2009) *Principles and Practice of Assessment in the Lifelong Learning Sector.* Exeter: Learning Matters

Tummons T (2007) *Assessing Learning in the Lifelong Learning Sector.* Exeter: Learning Matters

Williams J (2010) *Study Skills for PTLLS.* Exeter: Learning Matters

Websites

Assessment methods – www.brookes.ac.uk/services/ocsd/2_learntch/methods.html

Data Protection Act 1998 & 2003 – regulatorylaw.co.uk/Data_Protection_Act_ 2003.html

Initial assessment – www.excellencegateway.org.uk/page.aspx?o=nav-resources&node =8436

In this chapter you will learn about:

- planning and preparing your micro-teach session:

  pre-service;

  in-service;

- peer feedback:

  giving feedback;

  receiving feedback;

- evaluating your micro-teach session.

Planning and preparing your micro-teach session

To demonstrate your skills and knowledge as a teacher you are required to deliver a session either to your peers (pre-service) or in your place of work (in-service). This gives you the opportunity to put theory into practice. It will usually be for a minimum of 15 or 30 minutes and you will be observed by your teacher or an assessor. The date and time will be agreed in advance of your session. It would be useful, prior to your delivery to see the observation checklist they will be using, which will help you to know what they are looking for and enable you to ask any questions beforehand. Your observer might make a visual recording of your session which you can view in your own time. This will enable you to see things you were not aware of; for example, saying *erm*, using a lot of hand gestures or not using much eye contact. You should be told in advance if you are being recorded; try not to be put off by it, but embrace it as a way of developing yourself further.

You will need to prepare a session plan in advance which should have a clear aim (what you want your learners to achieve) which is then broken down into objectives (how your learners will achieve your aim). Objectives should be measurable to enable you to see that learning has taken place. The term 'learning outcomes' is often used now instead of 'objectives'; these are an expression of what your learner can do once learning has taken place, and may be longer in terms of time than objectives are.

Objectives should always be SMART.

- **S**pecific – are they clearly defined?

- **M**easurable – can they be met?

- **A**chievable – are they possible?

- **R**ealistic – do they relate to the aim?

- **T**ime bound – can they be met in the time?

Examples of SMART objectives include: *create, demonstrate, describe, explain* and *state*. Objectives which are not SMART include: *appreciate, attempt, discuss, understand* and *reflect*. When teaching, you should know which objectives you will expect your learners to achieve, as SMART objectives will enable you to assess their achievements. Objectives which are not SMART are more difficult to assess.

You will need to design in advance any activities, handouts, resources, presentations and assessments you will use. Make sure these are relevant to your aim and meet the objectives or learning outcomes you want your learners to achieve. You should also check them for spelling, grammar and punctuation errors and ensure text and pictures represent all aspects of society.

Have a trial run through to check your timings and have a contingency plan in case anything goes wrong. Make sure you have all the necessary equipment, resources and stationery, and check in advance that everything is working. You may want to rearrange the area beforehand to suit your subject, and you will need to tidy up and clear the area at the end. Setting up and clearing away are outside of the observed time.

You should create and use a session plan; a pro-forma can be found in Appendix 9 if you don't have one already. You should plan to have an introduction, a middle section and an ending to your delivery.

The introduction

You may feel nervous as you will be observed. However, try to imagine you are playing a role and this should help your confidence. You are the teacher in this situation and must not let any personal issues interfere with this. Don't state that you are nervous as it probably won't show to your learners. Stand tall and speak a little louder and slower than normal, as being anxious or nervous may make you speak faster. If you feel you are shaking, it is highly likely no one will notice this. If your mind suddenly goes blank, take a couple of deep breaths for a few seconds to help you refocus – it might seem a long time to you but it won't to your learners. You will need to establish a rapport with your learners, engage, interact and motivate them to make them feel at ease.

Keep your session plan handy as a prompt, ticking off aspects as you progress. If you feel you might forget something, use a highlight pen beforehand to mark key words which you can see quickly to prompt you. Introduce yourself, your aim and the objectives or learning outcomes (you might like to keep these on display throughout your session – perhaps on a piece of flipchart paper on the wall). Use eye contact with all your learners, and standing rather than sitting will help your confidence and voice projection. If you are writing on a board, try to do this at an angle so as not to turn your back on the group. If you are using presentation software, try not to have too much information on each slide, and look at the group as you talk through your points, rather than at the screen. A wireless slide presenter is a useful gadget to have as it enables you to move around the room, clicking it to advance the slides, rather than standing next to the computer and tapping a key. Keep things simple, don't try to achieve too much yourself, or expect too much of your learners. If this is the first time you have met your learners, you might want to carry out a short icebreaker with them or ask them to introduce themselves to you. You may not have time to agree any ground rules; however, you could state that you expect mobile phones to be switched off. You could ask your learners if they have any prior knowledge of your subject; if so, you can draw on their experiences throughout your session. You might like to encourage your learners to ask questions if they need to clarify any points and you could state that you will give a handout at the end which summarises your session.

The middle section

You should plan to use a variety of activities to reach all learning styles and retain motivation. Repeating important points will reinforce learning: this may be the first time your learners have heard or seen something and repetition will help them remember. Summarise and recap regularly and ask open questions to check knowledge. Try to use names when talking to your learners and include everyone in the group; don't just focus on a particular learner who you know can give you the correct answers. Open questions begin with *who, what, when, where, why* and *how*. Using closed questions, for example, *Are you all okay?* or *Do you have any questions?*, will usually result in *Yes* or *No* and does not help you ascertain their learning. As your learners answer any questions, remember to acknowledge these with praise and constructive feedback.

Try to vary your delivery and allow yourself time to explain points, followed by a practical activity for your learners to carry out. This enables them to draw on their own knowledge and experience and to work together either in pairs or small groups. You need to manage all activities carefully and set a time limit for each, reminding them when the time is nearly up. Depending upon your learners, you could let them decide who they will work with. However, letting them decide for themselves will take up valuable time. You might like to plan ahead who will work with whom and be assertive when you state this. The timing of activities needs to be followed carefully; if you are only delivering a 15-minute session you may not have time for group activities. If you do set activities, think what you will be doing while your learners are working: wandering around the room and observing or asking questions shows you are in control. Longer sessions benefit from a mixture of formal input from you, group activities, demonstrations and questions to ensure all learning styles are met.

You will find the time will go really quickly: be prepared to adapt your timings if necessary; for example, if the group activity is going really well, you could give your learners a little longer. Always inform them of any time limits or extensions to an activity and let them know how long they have left, at various points. If your formal input is not being received well you could move on to an activity or a discussion. Have a spare activity or some open questions planned just in case you do have time to fill.

The ending

This is a summary of your aim and the objectives or learning outcomes that have been covered in the session. You might like to ask your learners if they have any questions. However, they might either be silent, or have lots of questions, which will then impede upon your time. Issuing a handout is a good way of summarising the session content and will enable your learners to read it afterwards. You could add useful textbooks and websites for learners to research your topic further if they wish. Give the handout to your learners at the end of the session as you summarise, otherwise they will be looking at it during the session, which can cause disruption. A short quiz or multiple choice test is a good way to check knowledge if you have time and acts as an assessment activity. If you find you have covered everything and have spare time, you could ask each member of the group to state one thing they feel they have learnt from the session. This is a good way of filling in spare time if necessary, and shows you what has been learnt. If you are unsure of how to end your session, simply say *Thank you*: this will indicate to your group you have finished.

Do tidy the area when you finish, clean any boards you have used and close down any presentation equipment.

Level 4 micro-teach

If you are taking the PTLLS Award at level 4 you will need to demonstrate skills and knowledge appropriate to that level. For example, your session plan will need to be extremely thorough, follow a logical sequence and be planned in detail, with examples of embedding the functional skills of English, maths and information communication technology (ICT). The individual needs of your learners will need to be taken into account; for example, learning styles and different levels of ability. You should be aware of all the factors affecting your planning, delivery and assessment such as learner needs, the environment, resources and facilities, and also take into account equality and diversity, health and safety, and any relevant guidelines, codes of practice and legislation.

Timings for activities will need to be meticulous and you should be able to deal with any situations as they arise, particularly regarding disruption and behaviour. A mixture of delivery styles, activities and assessment methods should be used to engage your learners. Handouts should be of a high quality without any errors, and be issued at an appropriate time. There should be regular recaps to reinforce learning. You should demonstrate confidence in your subject and be able to answer any questions asked, communicating appropriately. Assessments should be varied and include open questions to each learner, allowing them all to participate. Feedback should be specific and developmental.

Communication is important, both verbal and non-verbal. You should remain conscious of your body language and the way you speak; for example, voice projection and clarity, pace, language and jargon used. You need to remain focused and listen to your learners, answering any questions as they arise. If you don't know the answer, say you will find out, and make sure you do.

Using a variety of delivery methods and incorporating ICT such as an interactive whiteboard will demonstrate your skills at using equipment to its best effect to engage and motivate your learners.

Pre-service

As a pre-service teacher you will be delivering to a group of your peers who will become your learners for the session. You will probably be in the same environment you have been learning in, or a central meeting point if you have been studying through a distance learning programme. Hopefully you will have met your peers previously and feel comfortable delivering to them; if not, it would be useful to talk to them beforehand to help everyone relax. While your micro-teach will be in a safe environment that you are probably familiar with, it is essentially a simulation as you are not teaching real learners who are taking a qualification. Even though it is a simulation, you may feel nervous and may have changed your mind a few times beforehand about what you will teach. Talk to your observer in advance about your ideas, and once you have decided on a suitable topic, try not to change your mind again but prepare your session plan. You could show your session plan to your observer a few days prior to your delivery to gain appropriate feedback. Having a practice run though at home with friends or family will help you plan your timings. You might also need to book some specialist equipment in advance or inform your peer group of anything they need to bring; for example, special clothing. You might want to check any prior knowledge of your peers in advance of the session or to inform them of the subject you will teach. You should have been told the date and time in advance, how long your session should last and whether you will be recorded.

If you are due to deliver after someone else, you will probably be thinking about your own delivery rather than focusing upon theirs. Try not to do this as it will make your nerves worse. Being well prepared and having self-confidence should help alleviate any worries.

Prior to your delivery, set up the area, check all equipment and move any tables and chairs as necessary (you might need help doing this) to ensure all your peers can see and hear you. Have a pen and your session plan somewhere close by to refer to regularly. A clock or a watch in a visible place will help you keep track of time. This should all be done prior to your timed session commencing. When you start, introduce yourself and your aim. You might like to ask if anyone has any prior knowledge of the subject you are delivering if you have not had the opportunity to do this beforehand. A useful question could be *Has anyone done this before?* This will help you include their experiences when asking questions and facilitating group activities. You may find your peers are very supportive during your micro-teach session and they might give you a round of applause at the end. Some useful hints and tips for micro-teaching can be found in Appendix 3.

In-service

You probably have some experience already of teaching, therefore delivering a session to your own learners should be fairly straightforward. However, as you will be observed you may feel nervous or anxious.

Your session might last longer than the time your observer will be present; they might therefore miss the beginning or ending and arrive part-way through. You should try to plan the session to allow yourself time to talk to your observer either before or afterwards. This will enable you to justify any aspects they have missed, to discuss your delivery and to receive feedback.

In preparation for your observed delivery, you might like to ask your subject mentor to observe one of your sessions and give you feedback. You could also observe your mentor or another colleague in the same subject area to see how they teach; you might pick up some useful ideas and information. Observing a teacher of a different subject from your own might give you some innovative ideas for your own subject.

The session you are delivering may be one of many, for which you will have a scheme of work to follow. You may want to introduce the observer to the group and state they are observing you, not them. Having a stranger in the room might lead to some behaviour issues. If so, you must deal with these as soon as they arise and in a professional manner. Your observer might be seeing the very first session of a programme, in which case you will have several administrative duties to perform, including an induction to the programme, icebreaker and the setting of ground rules. If you are being observed during one of several sessions, you will need to take the register and include a link to the last session with time for learner questions during your introduction.

At the end of your session you need to link to the next session (if applicable) and set any homework or extension activities for higher-level learners. Before your learners leave the room, make sure they tidy their work areas.

If this is the last session of a programme, you will need to incorporate some sort of evaluation activity to obtain feedback from your learners regarding their experiences. Your organisation may have a standard pro-forma for this or you could design your own. Some useful hints and tips for micro-teaching can be found in Appendix 3.

Peer feedback

Feedback is about helping someone learn from their actions or behaviour; it is not criticism, which is just a person's judgment or reaction to something, often said without careful thought. Feedback should always be given in a manner which will help the receiver become more effective in the future. Feedback is information and constructive opinions, not an instruction list and it will be up to the person receiving it if they wish to do anything with it. Good feedback is an offer of helpful information not a judgment of personality, character or potential.

Throughout your time attending a PTLLS Award programme you will have been carrying out various activities with your peers and giving each other feedback. You might have delivered some mini-sessions and received feedback from your teacher as well as your peers. Sometimes, your peers may be more negative when giving you feedback as they are not yet as skilled as your teacher at being constructive when giving it. Try not to take any negative comments personally: your peers are just saying what they see; hopefully their feedback skills will improve as the programme progresses. Alternatively, you might feel the feedback from your peers is quite helpful. Feedback should always include something positive or constructive, as well as any points for development.

One or more of your peers will give you feedback at the end of your taught session. This might be verbal or written depending upon how much time there is. They should also give you a form with written feedback on which you can look at afterwards to help you evaluate your session.

Level 4 feedback

If you are taking the PTLLS Award at level 4 you will need to explain different methods of giving feedback; for example, verbal or written, formal or informal. You will also need to demonstrate good practice in giving feedback to your peers if you are pre-service, or to your learners if you are in-service. This good practice should come from your ability to give feedback in a confident manner and in a way that leaves your recipient feeling they have benefited from it.

Different feedback methods include the following.

- Descriptive – examples of what could be improved and why; this can be written or verbal and is usually formal.

- Evaluative – statements such as *well done* or *good*. This method does not offer helpful or constructive advice; it can be written or verbal and is usually informal.

Descriptive feedback lets you describe what your recipient has done, how they have achieved the required outcomes and what they can do to progress further. It enables you to provide opportunities for them to make any adjustments or improvements to reach a particular standard.

Evaluative feedback might be good for your recipient to hear; for example, *well done Pete*. However, it does not give them the opportunity to know *what* was done well or *how* they could improve.

Giving feedback

Giving feedback is part of achieving the PTLLS Award and you may find it hard to do at first. If you have not had much experience, you might find you are being rather negative, critical or even worried your peers or learners might not like you as a result. You might have had negative feedback given to you in the past and this could influence the way you give it to others. Feedback is based on interaction and communication between people and some are better than others at giving it. Thinking carefully before speaking and considering what you have seen and heard will help you focus upon positive points and aspects for future development.

When giving feedback to others you need to be aware it could affect their self-esteem and whether they continue with the programme or not. The quality of feedback received can be a key factor in their progress and the ability to learn new skills. Ongoing constructive feedback which has been carefully thought through is an indication of your interest in the person and of your intention to help them develop and do well in the future.

When giving feedback:

- own your statements by using the word *I* rather than *you*;

- begin with something positive; for example, *I really liked the confident manner in which you delivered your session*;

- be specific about what you have seen; for example, *I felt the way you explained the law of gravity was really interesting due to your knowledge and humour* or *I found the way you explained the law of gravity was rather confusing to me*;

- offer constructive, specific or developmental follow-on points; for example, *I feel I would have understood it better if you had broken the subject down into smaller stages*;

- end with something positive; for example, *I enjoyed your session, you had prepared well and came across as very organised and professional*.

Being constructive, specific and developmental with what you say, and owning your statements should help the recipient to focus upon what you are saying as they will hear how they can improve. If you don't have any constructive, specific or developmental follow-on points then don't create them just for the sake of it. Conversely, if you do have any negative points or criticisms, don't say *My only negative point is...* or *My only criticisms are...* It's much better to replace these words and say '*Some areas for development could be...* instead.

You also need to make sure you are not being ambiguous or vague and that there are no disruptions or interruptions from the group while you are speaking. You need to be factual regarding what you have seen and experienced, not just give your opinion. Bear in mind that what you say can help or hinder a person's progress and confidence. Starting with something positive will help their motivation; they are then likely to listen to what else you have to say which will aid their development. Starting with something negative can be demoralising and they may not listen to what else is said. Negative comments can have a more powerful impact than positive ones. If you do need to give negative feedback, always back this up with specific suggestions as to how the person can improve.

Feedback should be a two-way process, allowing a discussion to take place to clarify any points. Consider your tone of voice and take into account any non-verbal signals; you may need to adapt your feedback if you see someone is becoming uncomfortable. Be aware of your own body language, facial expressions and tone of voice and don't use confrontational words or words likely to cause offence.

After starting with something positive, state what could be improved or changed, and finish on a positive note – this is known as the 'praise sandwich'. Use the person's name to make the feedback feel more personal, allow pauses for them to assimilate the information and ask if they have any questions at the end in case they need to clarify anything. Once you have given your feedback, you could ask them how they felt about your comments as this will give you some pointers for your own development.

Not every individual in the group will give feedback after each micro-teach session. Depending upon the amount of time, one person might give verbal feedback and the others will give written feedback.

If you are writing your feedback, this will probably be read at a later time; therefore you need to appreciate that how you write it may not be how it is read. It is easy to interpret words or phrases differently from those intended. Statements such as *well done* or *good* don't say *what* was well done or good or *how* it can be improved for the future.

The feedback you are giving is only your opinion. The observer will also be giving feedback and should clarify any points you have raised to ensure the person you have given feedback to does not feel demoralised. He or she may also give you feedback on how you have given feedback to your peers, to help you improve your own skills. If you can give feedback in a skilful manner, the others in the room will also learn from and benefit by what you have said. Peer assessment and constructive feedback have a valuable contribution to make to everyone's learning and development within the group.

The advantages of giving constructive feedback are that it:

● creates opportunities for clarification and discussion;

● emphasises progress rather than failure;

● helps improve confidence and motivation;

● identifies further learning opportunities or any action required.

Your observer should have planned who will be giving feedback to whom to enable everyone to focus carefully upon the relevant individual's session. You might be given a form to complete or you could use the peer observation and feedback pro-forma in Appendix 4.

Receiving feedback

Receiving feedback can sometimes be difficult as people often think it will be negative or critical. If one of your peers gives you negative feedback, you might feel your self-esteem is in question and want to be defensive or argumentative. If this happens, listen to what they say, but remember it is their opinion and your observer will also give you feedback which may differ from this. Just say *I'll take your comments on board* rather than arguing. Conversely, you might receive really good feedback and not know how to react. If this is the case, simply say *Thank you for your comments*.

When receiving feedback, whether from your peers or observer, you need to listen carefully, focusing on the positive and any negative or constructive points. The feedback from your observer should be given skilfully to help you realise what you did well and what you could improve upon for the future to reach your full potential. It will enable you to compare how you think you are doing with what others think, as how you perceive your own actions is often very different from how others do.

You might have had previous experiences of unhelpful or unjustified feedback which has had a negative effect upon your progress. This could have been due to the person reacting personally rather than professionally by not carefully considering what they will say or how they will say it.

Once you have finished your micro-teach session, you might be so relieved or busy packing away that you don't fully take on board what is being said to you. Listen carefully and ask questions to clarify any points you are unsure of. Try not to interrupt or become defensive when receiving feedback and don't take anything personally: the feedback will be given to help you improve.

You will receive a completed checklist or be given written feedback from your observer as well as from your peers. These can be used to inform your self-evaluation process.

Evaluating your micro-teach session

You may need to complete a self-evaluation form after delivering your micro-teach session, and an example pro-forma can be found in Appendix 5. This is similar to the peer feedback form and will enable you to compare your own and your peers' comments. Evaluating your own delivery is an important aspect of your learning and development. You might think you have done really well, but others may have given you some helpful advice during the feedback process which could improve your future teaching and personal development. You may even have received comments you had not considered and can therefore use these to help you improve or change things.

If your session has been recorded, you should view this as soon as possible and read your observer's feedback and peer feedback forms to help you evaluate how your session went. The forms and recording media can be placed in your portfolio as evidence of achievement.

When evaluating yourself, consider your strengths, areas for development and any action and improvements required from a teaching perspective and your subject knowledge. You also need to justify the reasons for your choice of teaching and learning approaches and resources you used. After your session, you might feel you used too many handouts or relied on presentation equipment too much.

Some questions to ask yourself include the following.

- How did I feel after I delivered my session?

- Did I deliver within the time or did I have to adjust/change anything?

- How do I know if my group learnt something as a result of my delivery?

- Why did I choose the teaching/learning methods I used?

- Did anything go wrong – if so, what did I do or could I do in the future to ensure this does not happen again?

- How did my session meet the needs of the group and individuals?

- What would I do differently next time?

- How can I use the feedback received to improve for the future?

At the end of the PTLLS Award programme you might find it useful to produce a personal profile and action plan. This is a statement of your overall development and what your strengths are. You can review your role at this time and set yourself an action plan; for example, if you are pre-service what will you do now to obtain a teaching position? If you are in-service you might consider your continuing professional development (CPD) in your subject area or how you will progress to other teaching qualifications such as the Certificate in Teaching in the Lifelong Learning Sector (CTLLS) if you are in an associate teaching role, or the Diploma in Teaching in the Lifelong Learning Sector (DTLLS) or Certificate in Education/Post Graduate Certificate in Education if you are in a full teaching role. By now you should have registered with the Institute for Learning (IfL) as this is a requirement under the Teaching Regulations 2007.

Level 4 evaluation

If you are taking the PTLLS Award at level 4 you will need to analyse the effectiveness of the resources you have used. You might have used too many different resources in a short space of time, which led to confusion. You also need to reflect on and evaluate the effectiveness of your own teaching and make recommendations for modification as appropriate. For example, the feedback from your peers stated you talked a lot and relied too much on an electronic presentation. You could in future use fewer slides in the presentation and engage your learners in a discussion or an activity. The self-evaluation form in Appendix 5 can be used as a starting point; however, you need to be more analytical than descriptive and state how and why you made the decisions you did and what you would change or modify.

Summary

In this chapter you have learnt about:

- planning and preparing your micro-teach session:

  pre-service;

  in-service.

- peer feedback:

  giving feedback;

  receiving feedback.

- evaluating your micro-teach session.

Theory focus

Books

Gravells A (2008) *Preparing to Teach in the Lifelong Learning Sector* (3rd edition). Exeter: Learning Matters

Reece I and Walker S (2007) *Teaching, Training and Learning; A Practical Guide* (6th edition). Tyne and Wear: Business Education Publishers Ltd

Wallace S (2007) *Teaching, Tutoring and Training in the Lifelong Learning Sector* (3rd edition). Exeter: Learning Matters

Williams J (2010) *Study Skills for PTLLS*. Exeter: Learning Matters

Websites

BBC – Feedback: giving and receiving – www.bbctraining.com/onlineCourse.asp?tID=2241

Institute for Learning – www.ifl.ac.uk

Oxford Learning Institute – giving and receiving feedback – www.learning.ox.ac.uk/rsv.php?page=319

Teaching Regulations 2007 – www.opsi.gov.uk/si/si2007/uksi_20072264_en_1

CHAPTER 7
THE PREPARING TO TEACH
IN THE LIFELONG LEARNING
SECTOR (PTLLS) AWARD

In this chapter you will learn about:

● level 3 and level 4 LLUK criteria;

● Awarding Organisation requirements;

● assessment methods.

Level 3 and level 4 LLUK criteria

The PTLLS Award can be thought of as a threshold licence to teach and is the start of the qualifications for your teaching career in the Lifelong Learning Sector. You will then have five years in which to achieve a relevant teaching qualification and gain your teaching status of Associate Teacher Learning and Skills (ATLS) or Qualified Teacher Learning and Skills (QTLS) depending upon your job role. You will need to register with the Institute for Learning (IfL, www.ifl.ac.uk), the professional body for teachers, trainers and assessors in the Lifelong Learning Sector.

Lifelong Learning UK (LLUK) is the employer-led sector skills council responsible for the professional development of staff working in the Lifelong Learning Sector in the United Kingdom. They have written the PTLLS Award criteria at both level 3 and level 4 to enable teachers to take the level appropriate to them at the commencement of their teaching career. As you progress through your programme of study, you will see that the learning outcomes for level 3 and level 4 are the same; the difference between the levels is expressed in the assessment criteria, enabling you meet the requirements at an appropriate level. For example, if you are taking level 3, you will explain *how* or *why* you do something; at level 4 you will *analyse* how or why you do it. If you are taking the level 4 assessments, you will need to carry out relevant research, reference your work to theorists and use an academic style of writing. If you are progressing to the Certificate or Diploma in Teaching in the Lifelong Learning Sector (CTLLS or DTLLS), you should be able to achieve the PTLLS Award at either level 3, or level 4 as both are acceptable. If you are progressing to the Certificate in Education or Post Graduate Certificate in Education, you may need to achieve the PTLLS Award at level 4. (If you have achieved at level 3, you might need to complete a bridging activity to demonstrate you can work at a higher level.) You will need to check with the training organisation you are enrolled at what they recommend. You might be taking the PTLLS Award as an embedded part of the CTLLS/DTLLS qualification or the Certificate in Education/ Post Graduate Certificate in Education. If so, the PTLLS unit will usually be delivered and assessed first.

Awarding Organisation requirements

Once you have enrolled to take the PTLLS Award at a training organisation, you will be registered with an Awarding Organisation. There are many Awarding Organisations; for example, City & Guilds, Edexcel and NCFE, who will each design assessment activities based upon the PTLLS Award criteria. The content of the programme you will be taking will be the same; however, the assessment requirements may differ depending upon which Awarding Organisation you are registered with and which level you are taking. Whichever Awarding Organisation you take your qualification with, it is a requirement that you are observed teaching a session. Your assessor will give you detailed feedback and your peers will also give you feedback. At some point you will also observe your peers and give them feedback.

You will need to keep all your work in a file or folder, often referred to as a portfolio. See Appendices 11 and 12 for examples of portfolio evidence. Unfortunately, there is a lot of plagiarism taking place due to the ease of access to information via the internet; therefore you may be asked to sign a statement that the work is your own. Awarding Organisations use different terminology for this, which might be known as:

- assessment record;
- authentication sheet;
- cover sheet;
- front sheet;
- record of achievement;
- signature sheet;
- unit declaration;
- unit summary;
- validation record.

Your work will be assessed and a sample internally and/or externally verified or moderated either during or at the end of your programme. When you have passed all the requirements, the training organisation you have enrolled with will apply for the certificate from the Awarding Organisation.

Assessment methods

Each Awarding Organisation will design its own assessment strategy for the PTLLS Award. While the learning outcomes of the qualification remain the same, no matter which Awarding Organisation you are registered with, the assessment methods may differ.

The following table shows some of the Awarding Organisations' assessment methods for the PTLLS Award. Information on each assessment method then follows in alphabetical order. You should check with the Awarding Organisation you are registered with for up-to-date information in case it has changed since the publication of this book – website details are available at the end of the chapter. If your Awarding Organisation is not listed here, you will need to ask the training organisation you have enrolled with for details.

Details of the main Awarding Organisations' assessment methods

Awarding Organisation	Assessment methods
Ascentis (formerly OCNW)	Assessment tasks Observation
CELTA *Certificate in English Language Teaching to Adults*	Assignments Observation
City & Guilds	Assignments – theory and practical tasks (including observation) OR Written questions and a reflective learning journal (including observation)
CYQ *Central YMCA Qualifications*	Essays, worksheets and theory paper Portfolio of evidence Reflective learning journal Observation
Edexcel	Assignments – theory and practical tasks (including observation) OR Portfolio of evidence and a reflective learning journal (including observation)
EDI	Assignments Observation
Future	Assignments – tasks and activities Assessment grids and checklists Self-evaluation record and action plan Portfolio of evidence Reflective learning journal Summative assessment record Observation
HABC *Highfield Awarding Body for Compliance*	Portfolio of evidence Observation
NCFE *(letters no longer an acronym)*	Portfolio of evidence Observation
NOCN *National Open College Network*	Assessment tasks: written description, case study Portfolio of evidence Observation
OCR *Oxford Cambridge and RSA*	A flexible approach whereby assignments (tasks and activities) can be designed by the training organisation Portfolio of evidence Observation
Other	*Other methods could include:* Online assessments Professional discussion Summative assessment record

Assessment grids and checklists

The Awarding Organisation you are registered with will have produced a grid or checklist which contains all the PTLLS Award assessment criteria. Either you or your assessor will complete these to show how you have achieved them. Your supporting evidence should clearly demonstrate how you have met the criteria at the level you aim to achieve. Your evidence will usually be placed in a portfolio.

Assignments and assessment tasks/activities

These will ensure that all the assessment criteria can be met through various tasks and activities which cover theory and practice. They might not be in the same order as the PTLLS Award learning outcomes; however, you should be able to complete all the requirements as you progress through your programme of study. There might be several theory or practical tasks or activities for you to complete which could include group discussions, presentations, essays and worksheets with time for self-reflection, feedback and evaluation of progress. Some written tasks and essays might have word counts to ensure you remain focused and specific with your responses, and all tasks will have deadline dates for submission. You will usually have to word-process your work in a professional font. However, if it is acceptable for you to hand write your responses, make sure your writing is legible and neatly written. Always check your spelling, grammar, punctuation and sentence structure. Try not to rely on your computer to check things for you as they don't often realise the context within which you are writing. If you are working at level 4, you must use academic writing and reference your work to relevant texts, journals, websites, etc. However, it is also good practice to do this at level 3. You will be given deadlines within which to submit your work; if you cannot keep to a date for any reason, make sure you discuss this with your assessor.

Essays, worksheets and theory paper

See the preceeding section on Assignments and assessment tasks/activities.

Observation

Your assessor will observe you teaching, whether this is a micro-teach session in front of your peers or an in-service session teaching your current learners. Your assessor will complete a checklist to ensure you meet all the observation criteria; it would be useful for you to obtain a copy of this in advance as this will enable you to see what your assessor is looking for. Your peers might also use a checklist and after your observation you will receive feedback from your assessor and your peers. A visual recording might be made of your session which you can view in your own time. This will enable you to see things you weren't aware of; for example, saying *erm* or not using much eye contact with learners. You need to consider these points and the feedback received when completing your self-evaluation and reflective learning journal. At some point you will also observe your peers and give them feedback, using a form or checklist to help you. While you are taking the PTLLS Award you may find it useful to arrange to observe your mentor if you are in-service, or a teacher in the same subject area as yourself if you are pre-service. This will help you see how they plan, prepare, deliver, assess and evaluate their session, giving you some useful ideas.

Online assessments

If you are taking the PTLLS Award programme via an online or distance learning programme, you will either email your responses to an assessor or upload your responses to a learning portal via a website. As you might not meet the person assessing your work, you need to stay in touch regularly and communicate any issues or concerns. You will still have to deliver a micro-teach session to a group of learners and be observed. Your assessor or an observer will either come to you at your own organisation if you are in-service, or will meet with you and others taking the programme at a suitable location. See the section on Assignments and assessment tasks/activities on page 59 for further details.

Portfolio of evidence

This is often in the form of a ring binder or folder with sections containing all your evidence to cover the assessment requirements. You could produce a front sheet with your personal details on, and follow this with your curriculum vitae or a personal statement. This information will help your assessor and verifier gain some background knowledge about you. You might be issued with an assessment record from the Awarding Organisation, which will be signed and dated as you progress. You might also need to sign and include a statement to confirm that the work you have produced is your own. Your portfolio will then contain all the evidence you have produced to fulfil the assessment criteria for each learning outcome of the PTLLS Award. This evidence will be in the form of written and practical work which should be cross-referenced to the assessment criteria. See Appendices 11 and 12 for examples of evidence. When producing this evidence, consider quality not quantity. Your assessor's observation and feedback notes should also be included as proof of your achievements. If you have been referred for any aspect, you will need to include your original and revised work.

Professional discussion

A professional discussion is a conversation with your assessor in which you will justify how you have achieved the assessment criteria. It could be used if you have completed a written task or activity and met most but not all of the assessment criteria. Having a professional discussion with your assessor is a good way to demonstrate you have now met the criteria without having to rewrite your work.

It can be used as a holistic assessment method as several criteria can be assessed at the same time. Your assessor will prompt you to explain how you have met the requirements and ask to see documentation which confirms this. Your assessor might make a recording of your conversation, either visual or aural, which can be kept as evidence of your achievement. Alternatively, your assessor might take notes during the discussion. Prior to the professional discussion taking place, you should agree with your assessor the nature of the conversation to enable you to prepare in advance. You may need to bring along examples of teaching materials you have prepared and used. When you are having the professional discussion try to remain focused, don't digress but be specific with your responses. At the end of the discussion, make sure you know which assessment criteria you have achieved, and which you still need to accomplish.

Questions – written and oral

You may need to produce answers to written questions which will be based around the assessment criteria. See the section on Assignments and assessment tasks/activities on page 59 for more information.

You might also be asked oral questions by your assessor, who will note down your responses or record your conversation. If you have answered a written question and met most but not all of the assessment criteria, your assessor might ask some oral questions to ensure you have the relevant skills and knowledge.

Reflective learning journal

Writing a reflective learning journal throughout your programme of study will help you focus upon your learning and development, enabling you to put theory into practice. You might be given a pro-forma to use, you could write in a diary or a notebook, or use the pro-forma in Appendix 10. When you write, make sure your work is legible as your assessor will need to read and understand it. Try to reflect upon your experiences by analysing as well as describing them and be as specific as possible as to how your experiences have met the PTLLS Award assessment criteria. You could annotate your writing with the criteria such as 1.1, 1.2, etc., to show which criteria you feel you have achieved. Don't just write a chronological account of events; consider what worked well, or didn't work, and how you could do something differently given the opportunity. If you are working at level 4, you should reference your work to reflective theorists. For example:

> Today I taught a group of 15 learners who were very disruptive. I introduced the topic at the beginning and most of them were talking over me. I tried shouting but this didn't have any effect. What I should have done was remain silent straight away until all the learners looked at me. This is based on Schön D (1983) – reflection in action. This would have gained their attention and enabled me to remind them of the ground rules regarding disruption. Next time I will display the ground rules on the wall and remind the group of these before we commence. Based on Schön (ibid) – reflection on action.

Reflection should become a part of your everyday activities and enable you to look at things in detail that you perhaps would not ordinarily do. There may be events you would not want to change or improve if you felt they went well. If this is the case, reflect as to why they went well and use similar situations in future sessions. As you become more experienced at reflective writing, you will see how you can make improvements to benefit your learners.

Self-evaluation record and action plan

This is a pro-forma for you to complete at the end of your teaching session. Your assessor might also complete a marking grid and observation record to ensure you have met the PTLLS Award requirements. Your responses and evidence should clearly demonstrate how you have met the criteria at the level you wish to achieve. The action plan will help you focus upon the skills, knowledge and understanding required for your personal development. You need to focus upon what you have learnt and how you have put this into practice, relating this to the skills, knowledge and understanding required for your development. Your evidence will usually be placed in a portfolio.

Summative assessment record

This is a pro-forma, rather like the ones in Appendices 11 and 12, and involves you stating how you have met the assessment criteria of the five learning outcomes. You will complete this to state how you have met each of the assessment criteria, or write a reference number which relates to the location of your evidence. Your responses and evidence should clearly demonstrate how you have met the assessment criteria at the level you wish to achieve. Your evidence will usually be placed in a portfolio.

All the work you produce towards achieving the five learning outcomes of the PTLLS Award will be assessed, no matter which methods have been used. As you work through the unit requirements you will be informed regularly of your progress by your assessor and you should have the opportunity to discuss any issues or concerns.

Summary

In this chapter you have learnt about:

- level 3 and level 4 LLUK criteria;

- Awarding Organisation requirements;

- assessment methods.

Theory focus

Books

Gravells A (2008) *Preparing to Teach in the Lifelong Learning Sector* (3rd edition). Exeter: Learning Matters

Williams J (2010) *Study Skills for PTLLS*. Exeter: Learning Matters

LLUK (2006) *New overarching professional standards for teachers, tutors and trainers in the Lifelong Learning Sector*. London: Skills for Business

Schön D (1983) *The Reflective Practitioner*. San Francisco: Jossey-Bass

Websites

Ascentis – www.ocnw.com

CELTA – www.celta.org.uk

City & Guilds – www.cityandguilds.com

CYQ – www.cyq.org.uk

Edexcel – www.edexcel.com

EDI – www.ediplc.com

Future – www.futurequals.com

HABC – www.highfieldabc.com

Institute for Learning – www.ifl.ac.uk

Lifelong Learning UK – www.lluk.org

NCFE – www.ncfe.org.uk

NOCN – www.nocn.org.uk

OCR – www.ocr.org.uk

Criteria and self-audit level 3
Preparing to teach in the lifelong learning sector – self-audit

Learning outcomes The learner will:	Assessment criteria The learner can:	List of evidence which covers the assessment criteria:	Work required to meet the assessment criteria:
1. Understand own role, responsibilities and boundaries of role in relation to teaching	1.1 Explain own role and responsibilities, and boundaries of own role as a teacher 1.2 Identify key aspects of relevant current legislative requirements and codes of practice within a specific context 1.3 Identify other points of referral available to meet the potential needs of learners 1.4 Identify issues of equality and diversity, and ways to promote inclusion 1.5 Explain the need for record keeping		
2. Understand appropriate teaching and learning approaches in the specialist area	2.1 Identify and demonstrate relevant approaches to teaching and learning in relation to the specialist area 2.2 Explain ways to embed elements of functional skills in the specialist area 2.3 Justify selection of teaching and learning approaches for a specific session		

Learning outcomes The learner will:	Assessment criteria The learner can:	List of evidence which covers the assessment criteria:	Work required to meet the assessment criteria:
3. Demonstrate session planning skills	3.1 Plan a teaching and learning session which meets the needs of individual learners 3.2 Justify selection of resources for a specific session		
4. Understand how to deliver inclusive sessions which motivate learners	4.1 Explain ways to establish ground rules with learners which underpin appropriate behaviour and respect for others 4.2 Use a range of appropriate and effective teaching and learning approaches to engage and motivate learners 4.3 Explain and demonstrate good practice in giving feedback 4.4 Communicate appropriately and effectively with learners 4.5 Reflect on and evaluate the effectiveness of own teaching		
5. Understand the use of different assessment methods and the need for record keeping	5.1 Identify different assessment methods 5.2 Explain the use of assessment methods in different contexts, including reference to initial assessment 5.3 Explain the need for record keeping in relation to assessment		

Criteria and self-audit level 4
Preparing to teach in the lifelong learning sector – self-audit

Learning outcomes The learner will:	Assessment criteria The learner can:	List of evidence which covers the assessment criteria	Work required to meet the assessment criteria
1. Understand own role, responsibilities and boundaries of role in relation to teaching	1.1 Review own role and responsibilities, and boundaries of own role as a teacher 1.2 Summarise key aspects of relevant current legislative requirements and codes of practice within a specific context 1.3 Review other points of referral available to meet the potential needs of learners 1.4 Discuss issues of equality and diversity, and ways to promote inclusion 1.5 Justify the need for record keeping		
2. Understand appropriate teaching and learning approaches in the specialist area	2.1 Identify, adapt and use relevant approaches to teaching and learning in relation to the specialist area 2.2 Evaluate a range of ways to embed elements of functional skills in the specialist area 2.3 Evaluate the teaching and learning approaches for a specific session		

Learning outcomes The learner will:	Assessment criteria The learner can:	List of evidence which covers the assessment criteria:	Work required to meet the assessment criteria:
3. Demonstrate session planning skills	3.1 Plan a teaching and learning session which meets the needs of individual learners 3.2 Evaluate how the planned session meets the needs of individual learners 3.3 Analyse the effectiveness of the resources for a specific session		
4. Understand how to deliver inclusive sessions which motivate learners	4.1 Analyse different ways to establish ground rules with learners which underpin appropriate behaviour and respect for others 4.2 Use a range of appropriate and effective teaching and learning approaches to engage and motivate learners 4.3 Explain different methods of giving feedback 4.4 Demonstrate good practice in giving feedback 4.5 Communicate appropriately and effectively with learners 4.6 Reflect on and evaluate the effectiveness of own teaching, making recommendations for modification as appropriate		
5. Understand the use of different assessment methods and the need for record keeping	5.1 Review a range of different assessment methods 5.2 Evaluate the use of assessment methods in different contexts, including reference to initial assessment 5.3 Justify the need for record keeping in relation to assessment		

Micro-teach: hints and tips

- Find out when and where you will be, what resources are available and how long your session will last

- Prepare your session plan in advance, ensuring you have an aim and SMART objectives (or learning outcomes), and that you have a beginning, middle and end to your delivery

- Try not to change your mind too many times about what to teach

- Keep things simple – don't try to achieve too much

- Practise your session at home in front of friends/family: they may ask questions which will help you plan your responses

- Check your timings are realistic, have an extra activity in case you have spare time, or know what you can leave out if you run short of time

- Arrive early to check the room, equipment and resources

- Set up the area to suit your topic, so that everyone can see and hear you – you might need to move tables, chairs and equipment

- Be prepared, be organised, be professional and dress appropriately

- Have a watch handy, or position a clock somewhere so that you can keep track of the time; have spare pens, paper, board marker, etc.

- Have a contingency plan in case anything goes wrong or is not available; for example, handouts as an alternative in case the presentation equipment stops working

- Introduce yourself, your aim and the objectives (or learning outcomes). It is useful to have these visible throughout your session, perhaps on flipchart paper – check with your observer if you need to use an icebreaker or agree ground rules

- Present your topic confidently and include the group with questions and short activities, make use of resources such as ICT/board /flipchart /projector and/or presentation software

- Check slides and handouts for spelling/grammar/punctuation errors and ensure text and pictures represent all aspects of society

- Use names when speaking to individuals or asking questions and include everyone

- Use eye contact and stand tall, speak a little slower and louder than normal

- If you set a group activity, think about what you will be doing while they are active and set time limits

- Check learning has taken place by asking open questions or carrying out some form of assessment activity; for example, a worksheet or quiz. Always confirm achievement (or otherwise) and give constructive feedback

- Provide a handout to summarise your session with further details; for example, books, websites, etc.

- Recap your aim and objectives (or learning outcomes) in your summary

- If you are not sure what to do when you finish, simply say *Thank you*

- Tidy up afterwards

Prior to delivering your session, ask to see your observer's micro-teaching observation checklist to get an idea of what they will be looking for.

You will receive feedback from your observer and your peers; you should take this into consideration when completing your self-evaluation form.

Notes

Peer observation and feedback pro-forma

Name of teacher: **Date:**   **Name of observer:**

Did the teacher?	Yes/No	Examples
introduce themselves and create a rapport with the learners		
state the aim and objectives (*or learning outcomes*)		
prepare adequately; for example, equipment/resources/handouts		
communicate clearly		
appear confident and professional		
ask open questions to check knowledge		
involve and include everyone during the session		
demonstrate their subject knowledge		
use a range of teaching and learning approaches		
take into account: health and safety equality and diversity learning styles functional skills Every Child Matters		
check that learning took place		
summarise their session and refer to the objectives (*or learning outcomes*)		
tidy the area afterwards		

Strengths	
Areas for development	
Action and improvements required	

Self-evaluation pro-forma

Name: **Date of taught session:**

Did I?	Yes/No	Examples
introduce myself and create a rapport with the learners		
state my aim and objectives (*or learning outcomes*)		
prepare adequately; for example, equipment/resources/handouts		
communicate clearly		
appear confident and professional		
ask open questions to check knowledge		
involve and include everyone during the session		
demonstrate subject knowledge		
use a range of teaching and learning approaches		
take into account: health and safety; equality and diversity; learning styles; functional skills; Every Child Matters		
check that learning took place		
summarise my session and refer to the objectives (*or learning outcomes*)		
tidy the area afterwards		

Strengths	
Areas for development	
Action and improvements required	
Justification for choice of teaching and learning approaches/resources	

Rationale for micro-teach session

Do I have a logical beginning, middle and end to my session?	
How long will I allocate to each aspect of my session to ensure a mix of activities?	
What do I need to prepare in advance? (*room/resources/handouts, etc.*)	
Do any of my learners have any individual requirements? If so, how will I address these?	
How will I introduce my session? (*my name and aim*)	
What will the group learn? (*objectives or learning outcomes*)	
Will I need to incorporate an icebreaker or ground rules?	
How can I embed functional skills and Every Child Matters into my delivery (if applicable)?	
How will I deliver my session? (*methods to cover all learning styles*)	
What resources and activities will I use? (*take into account health and safety and equality and diversity*)	
How will I assess my learners' knowledge and/or skills? (*including initial assessment/prior knowledge*)	
What open questions can I ask to check knowledge?	
What will I do if I run out of time?	
What can I remove if I have overrun my time?	
How will I summarise my session?	
What will I do after my session?	
Have I completed a session plan pro-forma?	

Rationale for scheme of work

What is my subject? Am I confident/qualified to teach it? *If not, what can I do?*	
Who is the Awarding Organisation? Is a syllabus available? *If there isn't a syllabus, do I need to produce my own?*	
Do other staff teach the same learners? If so, can we communicate to ensure no duplication? Can I use expert speakers? Can we go on visits or outings?	
How many sessions will I be teaching and how long will they be? *(hypothetical if you are pre-service)*	
Are there any timetabling issues, e.g. bank or public holidays, room availability?	
Who are my learners? Numbers, ages, levels, special requirements? *(hypothetical if you are pre-service)*	
How will I address a variety of learning styles within my teaching?	
What teaching methods will I use? Am I able to use a range of activities/ICT?	
What is the overall aim of the programme? Can this be easily broken down into SMART objectives or learning outcomes?	
How can I deliver the syllabus content in a logical order or sequence?	
What will I cover in the first session? e.g. icebreaker, ground rules	
How can I break down the content into an introduction, main content and conclusion for each session?	
How can I embed functional skills, equality and diversity and Every Child Matters into my delivery?	

Are there any health and safety and/or environmental considerations?	
What handouts/resources will I need to create or adapt?	
What assessment materials will I need to use (*including initial assessment*) and how will I use them?	
What will I cover in the last session e.g. an evaluation, summary of the programme?	
How will I evaluate my delivery?	

Notes

Scheme of work pro-forma

Programme/Qualification	Group	Dates from:	to:
Number of sessions	Contact hours Non-contact hours	Venue	
Aim			

Integrate functional skills of English, maths and ICT where possible and the Every Child Matters outcomes

Dates	Objectives or learning outcomes	Activities and resources	Assessment

Session plan pro-forma

Teacher		Date		Venue	
Subject & level/ syllabus reference		Time & Duration		Number of learners	
Aim of session					
Group composition	*Consider differentiation, equality and diversity, individual learning needs and learning styles*				

Integrate functional skills of English, maths and ICT where possible and the Every Child Matters outcomes

Timing	Objectives or learning outcomes	Resources	Teacher activities	Learner activities	Assessment

Reflective learning journal pro-forma

Name   **Date**

Experience *significant event or incident*	
Describe *who, what, when, where*	
Analyse *why, how* *(impact on teaching and learning)*	
Revise *changes and/or improvements required*	

Examples of portfolio evidence – level 3

Learning outcomes The learner will:	Assessment criteria The learner can:	Example evidence: See the *guidance for evidencing competence sections of* *Chapters 1–5.*
1. Understand own role, responsibilities and boundaries of role in relation to teaching	1.1 Explain own role and responsibilities, and boundaries of own role as a teacher 1.2 Identify key aspects of relevant current legislative requirements and codes of practice within a specific context 1.3 Identify other points of referral available to meet the potential needs of learners 1.4 Identify issues of equality and diversity, and ways to promote inclusion 1.5 Explain the need for record keeping	1.1 An explanation of the roles and responsibilities of a teacher, along with example boundaries that might be encountered (linked to the training cycle or learning cycle). Job description and CV. 1.2 A list of legislation and codes of practice relevant to subject specialism, organisation and teaching role, with the key aspects of each stated. 1.3 A list of potential needs of learners along with relevant points of referral and support systems available such as people, agencies, organisations etc. 1.4 An explanation of what equality, diversity and inclusion mean, along with examples of how these could be promoted with learners. 1.5 An explanation as to why records are kept eg legislation and organisational requirements, along with some examples.
2. Understand appropriate teaching and learning approaches in the specialist area	2.1 Identify and demonstrate relevant approaches to teaching and learning in relation to the specialist area 2.2 Explain ways to embed elements of functional skills in the specialist area 2.3 Justify selection of teaching and learning approaches for a specific session	2.1 An explanation of relevant teaching and learning approaches which relate to the subject to be taught. Scheme of work, session plan, tutor observation and peer or learner feedback. 2.2 A statement of what functional skills are. Examples of how English, maths and ICT could be embedded within the subject to be taught. 2.3 A justification as to the reasons why the teaching and learning approaches have been selected for a specific session.
3. Demonstrate session planning skills	3.1 Plan a teaching and learning session which meets the needs of individual learners 3.2 Justify selection of resources for a specific session	3.1 Syllabus or qualification handbook. Rationale for scheme or work and micro teach session. Actual scheme of work and session plan showing how individual needs will be met eg differentiation for different levels, abilities and individual needs. Examples of resources and activities to be used. 3.2 A justification as to the reasons why the resources and activities were chosen for a specific session.

Learning outcomes The learner will:	Assessment criteria The learner can:	Example evidence: See the guidance for evidencing competence sections of Chapters 1–5.
4. Understand how to deliver inclusive sessions which motivate learners	4.1 Explain ways to establish ground rules with learners which underpin appropriate behaviour and respect for others 4.2 Use a range of appropriate and effective teaching and learning approaches to engage and motivate learners 4.3 Explain and demonstrate good practice in giving feedback 4.4 Communicate appropriately and effectively with learners 4.5 Reflect on and evaluate the effectiveness of own teaching	4.1 An explanation of what ground rules are, along with how these can be negotiated, discussed or imposed upon learners. An explanation of how behaviour and respect can be managed by the use of ground rules. A list of possible ground rules relevant to the subject to be taught along with any organisational requirements. 4.2 Session plan. Tutor observation checklist. Examples of resources and activities used. An explanation as to how the approaches engage and motivate learners. 4.3 Evidence of giving feedback to others eg completed peer observation and feedback pro-formas. Tutor observation checklist. 4.4 An explanation of the communication methods used with learners and how effective these were. Tutor observation checklist and completed peer observation and feedback pro-formas. 4.5 Completed self evaluation pro-forma. Reflective learning journals. A statement as to how effective teaching was. Action plan for self.
5. Understand the use of different assessment methods and the need for record keeping	5.1 Identify different assessment methods 5.2 Explain the use of assessment methods in different contexts, including reference to initial assessment 5.3 Explain the need for record keeping in relation to assessment	5.1 A list of different assessment methods eg observation, questions, quiz, etc. 5.2 An explanation of what initial assessment is and why it can be used to inform learning. An explanation of how the assessment methods in 5.1 above could be used in different situations and contexts eg to assess knowledge/skills/individual needs etc. 5.3 A list of assessment records with an explanation as to why they are used.

Examples of portfolio evidence – level 4

Learning outcomes The learner will:	Assessment criteria The learner can:	Example evidence: See the *guidance for evidencing competence* sections of Chapters 1–5. Statements should be produced using academic writing and referencing conventions.
1. Understand own role, responsibilities and boundaries of role in relation to teaching	1.1 Review own role and responsibilities, and boundaries of own role as a teacher 1.2 Summarise key aspects of relevant current legislative requirements and codes of practice within a specific context 1.3 Review other points of referral available to meet the potential needs of learners 1.4 Discuss issues of equality and diversity and ways to promote inclusion 1.5 Justify the need for record keeping	1.1 An explanation, review and consideration of the roles and responsibilities of a teacher, along with example boundaries that might be encountered (linked to the training cycle or learning cycle). Job description and CV. 1.2 A report summarising legislation and codes of practice relevant to the subject specialism, organisation and teaching role, with the key aspects of each stated. 1.3 A report regarding the potential needs of learners along with relevant points of referral and support systems available such as people, agencies, organisations etc. 1.4 An explanation and discussion of what equality, diversity and inclusion mean, along with examples of how these could be promoted with learners. A summary of relevant Equality and Diversity legislation and organisational policies and procedures. 1.5 A report justifying why records are kept eg legislation and organisational requirements, along with examples of the records a teacher would maintain.
2. Understand appropriate teaching and learning approaches in the specialist area	2.1 Identify, adapt and use relevant approaches to teaching and learning in relation to the specialist area 2.2 Evaluate a range of ways to embed elements of functional skills in the specialist area 2.3 Evaluate the teaching and learning approaches for a specific session	2.1 A report identifying relevant approaches to teaching and learning with examples which relate to the specialist. Evidence of adapting and using various approaches and resources. Scheme of work, session plan, tutor observation checklist and peer or learner feedback. 2.2 A report explaining what functional skills are and why they are needed. An evaluation of a range of ways to embed English, maths and ICT within the specialist subject. 2.3 A report evaluating why the teaching and learning approaches have been selected for a specific session.

Learning outcomes The learner will:	Assessment criteria The learner can:	Example evidence: See the *guidance for evidencing competence sections of chapters 1–5*. Statements should be produced using academic writing and referencing conventions
3. Demonstrate session planning skills	3.1 Plan a teaching and learning session which meets the needs of individual learners 3.2 Evaluate how the planned session meets the needs of individual learners 3.3 Analyse the effectiveness of the resources for a specific session	3.1 Syllabus or qualification handbook. Rationale for scheme or work and micro teach session. Detailed scheme of work and session plan showing how individual needs will be met eg differentiation for different levels, abilities and individual needs. Examples of resources and activities to be used. 3.2 An evaluation of the content of a specific session plan as to how the teaching and learning approaches chosen will meet the needs of individual learners. 3.3 A report analysing the effectiveness of the resources and activities used for a specific session. Tutor observation checklist, peer and learner feedback. Reflective learning journal.
4. Understand how to deliver inclusive sessions which motivate learners	4.1 Analyse different ways to establish ground rules with learners which underpin appropriate behaviour and respect for others 4.2 Use a range of appropriate and effective teaching and learning approaches to engage and motivate learners 4.3 Explain different methods of giving feedback 4.4 Demonstrate good practice in giving feedback 4.5 Communicate appropriately and effectively with learners 4.6 Reflect on and evaluate the effectiveness of own teaching, making recommendations for modification as appropriate	4.1 An explanation of what ground rules are, along with an analysis of how these can be negotiated, discussed or imposed upon learners. A report analysing how behaviour and respect can be managed by the use of ground rules. A list of possible ground rules relevant to the subject to be taught along with any organisational requirements. 4.2 Session plan. Tutor observation checklist. Examples of resources and activities used. A report as to how the approaches engaged and motivated learners. 4.3 A report regarding different methods of giving feedback along with the advantages and limitations of each. 4.4 Evidence of giving feedback to others eg completed peer observation and feedback pro-formas. Tutor observation checklist. 4.5 A report regarding effective communication. List of barriers to communication with possible solutions. An explanation of the communication methods used with learners and how effective these were. Tutor observation checklist and completed peer observation and feedback pro-formas. 4.6 Completed self evaluation pro-forma. Reflective learning journals. An evaluation as to how effective teaching was with recommendations for changes and modification of practice. Action plan for self.

5. Understand the use of different assessment methods and the need for record keeping	5.1 Review a range of different assessment methods	5.1 A report reviewing a range of different assessment methods along with the advantages and limitations of each.
	5.2 Evaluate the use of assessment methods in different contexts, including reference to initial assessment	5.2 A report evaluating the different contexts within which assessment can be used. An explanation of what initial assessment is, why it can be used with learners and how the results can be used to inform learning. Examples of initial assessment activities.
	5.3 Justify the need for record keeping in relation to assessment	5.3 A report justifying the need for assessment records eg legislation and organisational requirements. Examples of records with an explanation as to why and how they are used.

INDEX